# Amazing and Inspiring Women in History

## The Frontline of Feminist Revolution

D1520940

**Stella Renee Stuart**

# Table of Contents

# Introduction

What if every girl truly knew her worth, understood her rights, and felt empowered to shape her own destiny? How could we improve the world around us by encouraging all women to rise above adversity like the many inspirational women in history? Feminism is not just a movement; it is a powerful lens through which we can view the world, revealing the untapped potential and rights of women everywhere. These narratives take us on a journey toward equality and female empowerment.

The tale of feminism spans centuries and continents, yet its core still remains relevant today. To appreciate its significance, we must first look back at the extraordinary women and key moments that defined this movement. Picture Mary Wollstonecraft in the 18th century, boldly advocating for women's education against the backdrop of a world that largely denied them intellectual freedom. Her voice was among the first to question deeply established societal norms, setting the stage for generations of young girls and women who dared to imagine more.

Fast forward to contemporary figures like Malala Yousafzai, whose unwavering fight for girls' education continues to echo around the globe. Her story epitomizes the ongoing struggle for basic rights that many still confront, reminding us that the quest for gender equality remains unfinished. The journey from Wollstonecraft to Yousafzai is paved with the courage of countless others—women who took up the mantle of change despite immense opposition, forever altering the fabric of society in the process.

However, to understand feminism fully, we must recognize its diverse roots. It is a global movement filled with culture and diversity, each narrative contributing unique perspectives and challenges. Consider Sojourner Truth, whose powerful advocacy for racial and gender equality during the abolition movement transformed the American landscape. Her story shows us how feminism influences multiple aspects of our self-identity.

1

In Europe, Angela Merkel's leadership in modern politics highlights another aspect of the feminist influence. As Germany's first female Chancellor, Merkel navigated complex geopolitical landscapes, redefining what leadership could look like. These are just a few examples that can remind us of feminism and its dynamic force, encompassing voices and experiences from all walks of life. Throughout this book, we will be exploring these stories and many others, discovering how all these inspiring women have paved the way for us today.

When journeying through these past triumphs, it's important to remember the relevance of feminism today. In an era where women and girls continue to face systemic barriers, the lessons drawn from history become invaluable. We stand in a world where gender inequality is still present. Confronting these age-old prejudices alongside new challenges posed by rapidly changing societal norms can bring us a step closer to equality. Issues such as gender pay gaps, limited access to education, and the perpetuation of harmful stereotypes persist, emphasizing the urgency of sustained activism.

As you reflect on your personal life, you may recall instances where gender has shaped your experiences—when your voice was silenced or an opportunity overlooked simply due to your sex. These recollections that many of us share as women are part of a larger narrative that binds us to the past and propels us into the future. After reflecting on your own life as a woman, you'll find that understanding the stories of courageous women provides invaluable guidance and inspiration, offering strategies to navigate personal hurdles you may face and empowering you to advocate for broader change.

This book is crafted for readers like you—whether you're a woman seeking role models, a young girl eager to learn from pioneering feminists, or an activist committed to starting meaningful discussions around gender equality. Through compelling biographical accounts, we will explore how groundbreaking ideas and actions have sparked transformational shifts in societies worldwide.

As we venture through these narratives, I aim to honor the legacies of those who came before and share the knowledge necessary to forge our paths forward as empowered women. You will encounter tales of resilience and rebellion, of visionaries who envisioned possibilities beyond their circumstances. Each chapter builds upon the last, painting a vivid portrait of feminism as both a historical phenomenon and a living dialogue with the present.

In understanding these contributions, you can view yourself as part of a larger community striving for justice. By engaging with this text, you join a conversation that transcends borders and generations, one that invites us all to envision a world where gender no longer dictates destiny.

Whether you're encountering these stories for the first time or returning to familiar themes, we hope this exploration deepens your understanding and commitment to shaping a more equitable world. May this journey encourage you to stand confidently in your power, inspired by the legacy of those who blazed the trail before you.

# Chapter 1:
# Feminism: A Foundation Across Ages

Feminism has served as a powerful approach to advocating women's rights and gender equality throughout history. Its evolution reflects the struggles and triumphs of countless women who have fought against societal constraints to assert their presence and capabilities. This chapter discusses the roots of feminism, tracing its journey and showcasing what women from the past endured and the significance it's had on young girls today. By reading about the influential lives and works of historical figures like Mary Wollstonecraft, Sojourner Truth, Susan B. Anthony, Ada Lovelace, and Marie Curie, you can learn about the foundational principles that continue to inspire modern feminist movements. These narratives can encourage resilience, intellect, and passion that pave the way for future generations while challenging prevailing norms and advocating for change. Through this chapter, we'll start with the seminal contributions of Mary Wollstonecraft, whose bold arguments for women's education and autonomy in the 18th century laid the groundwork for feminist advocacy as we know it today.

# Mary Wollstonecraft's Fundamental Ideas

Mary Wollstonecraft (1759-1797) known for her pioneering work in advocating for women's rights and education. Her influential paper, "A Vindication of the Rights of Woman," published in 1792, challenged the societal norms of her time and laid the groundwork for future feminist movements.

Mary was born on April 27, 1759, in London, England. She was the second of seven children in her family. Growing up, Mary faced many challenges that shaped her thoughts and beliefs. Her father, Edward Wollstonecraft, was known to be an abusive and irresponsible man. He often drank too much and did not provide a stable home for his family. This led to financial difficulties, and Mary experienced the strains of poverty during her early years. This situation pushed her mother, Elizabeth, to take on the role of provider for the family, which was unusual for women at that time (The Editors of Encyclopedia Britannica, 2018).

As a child, Mary was exposed to both the struggles and the strengths of women. Her mother's determination to support her children deeply influenced Mary's outlook on life, demonstrating that women could also be strong and independent. Despite her difficult family dynamics, Mary was intelligent and learned quickly. She was encouraged to read, which was not always the case for girls in her time. She found solace and inspiration in books, which greatly expanded her horizons and fueled her desire for knowledge. Some of the authors she read included John Locke and Rousseau, who influenced her thinking about education and society.

Mary's education was less formal than that of many of her male contemporaries. The curriculum for girls in the 18th century was limited and focused more on domestic skills rather than intellectual development. However, Mary was determined to learn, and she pursued her studies with vigor. She took on the responsibility of teaching her younger siblings and recognizing the power of education to change lives. She believed that knowledge was essential for personal growth and empowerment, especially for women, who were often denied equal opportunities.

At the age of 19, Mary began to seek her own path. She worked as a governess, which allowed her to earn some income while continuing her quest for knowledge. Although this role was considered respectable for women, it presented its own set of challenges. Governesses were often isolated and had limited interaction with society. Mary used this time to reflect on her experiences and opinions about women's roles in society. She became increasingly aware of the restrictions placed on women and of how these limitations affected their lives (The editors of encyclopedia Britannica, 2018).

In her early twenties, Mary experienced personal loss when her mother passed away. This event had a profound impact on her and intensified her desire to advocate for women's rights. She realized that her mother's struggles were not unique but shared by many women. This realization motivated Mary to become a voice for those who were silenced. She began to take writing seriously, realizing that words could challenge the status quo and shed light on the injustices faced by women.

Mary's life took a significant turn when she moved to Ireland to work as a governess for a wealthy family. It was there that she met individuals who further inspired her, including philosophers and writers who shared her progressive views. She observed the contrast between the wealthy elite and the poor, deepening her understanding of social issues. Her experiences in Ireland fueled her passion for writing and her commitment to studying the politics of her time. She started to see writing as a way to express her thoughts and promote change.

After returning to England, Mary struggled to find her place. She faced many rejections in her early attempts to publish her work, both books and articles. Yet, her determination did not wane. Instead, she continued to refine her ideas and critiques about society, focusing especially on the treatment of women. Mary wanted to highlight that education was a right, not a privilege, for all individuals, regardless of their gender. She became an advocate for the idea that women should be educated to become rational beings capable of contributing to society.

As she gained more confidence in her writing, Mary began to connect with other intellectuals and reformers. These connections proved valuable, providing her with the support she needed to advance her career as a writer. She attended salons and discussions where progressive ideas were exchanged and cultivated. These gatherings allowed her to refine her thoughts and network with other thinkers who believed in equality and justice.

Mary Wollstonecraft's background, and childhood set the foundation for her future activism and writings. The tumultuous relationship with her father, the influence of her strong mother, and her early experiences shaped her into a critical thinker. Her exposure to education, literature, and social issues inspired her to address the inequities faced by women in her society. She became one of the first advocates for women's rights and a marked influence on future generations.

Throughout her life, Mary faced numerous obstacles, but she persevered. She transformed her experiences into a powerful narrative advocating for change. Her voice became a rallying point for those who believed in gender equality through her published work. Mary Wollstonecraft's childhood was not devoid of struggle, but it was these very struggles that ignited her passion for writing and social justice, paving the way for her impactful legacy.

Mary Wollstonecraft's groundbreaking work, "A Vindication of the Rights of Woman," stands as a foundational feminist thought. Published in 1792, this paper (87,000 words long and almost at book length) boldly challenged the societal norms of the time by advocating for the rights of women, particularly emphasizing the necessity of education and autonomy. Wollstonecraft's arguments laid the groundwork for future feminist movements, resonating through centuries as an enduring call for gender equality.

In her writings, Wollstonecraft critiqued the inadequate education offered to women of her era. She argued passionately that women's education was superficial, designed merely to make them pleasing companions to men rather than independent thinkers. This system left women confined to roles that limited their potential and stifled their intellectual growth (Sottosanti, 2023). Wollstonecraft contended that a robust education would empower women to engage fully with society, enabling them to cultivate reason and virtue—attributes she believed were essential for any human being.

Wollstonecraft's critique extended beyond education to encompass societal gender roles and expectations. She saw these as artificial constructs that served to maintain female subjugation. In her view, women were taught from birth to prioritize appearance and marriage over personal development and intellectual pursuits (Bestmann, 2018). This social conditioning not only impeded women's progress but also perpetuated their dependency on men. By comparing the state of women to slavery, Wollstonecraft highlighted the systemic nature of gender inequality, describing how societal norms degraded both women and men—the former by oppression and the latter by embodying false notions of superiority.

Wollstonecraft's ideas carried significant implications for later feminist movements. Her insistence on equal educational opportunities for women prefigured demands made during the suffrage movements in the 19th and early 20th centuries. Activists like Elizabeth Cady Stanton and Susan B. Anthony drew inspiration from Wollstonecraft's work, using her arguments to advocate for broader societal changes

(Sottosanti, 2023). The principles she set forth about women's rights and dignity provided a philosophical backbone for numerous campaigns aimed at dismantling patriarchal barriers.

Despite the passage of time, Wollstonecraft's theories continue to resonate in contemporary feminist discussions. The ongoing struggle for gender equality in education, employment, and society echoes her pioneering calls for reform. Today's feminists still grapple with issues such as wage gaps, underrepresentation in leadership roles, and cultural stereotypes—all areas touched upon by Wollstonecraft's writings. By examining her thoughts alongside modern challenges, we see a clear line connecting past and present efforts towards female autonomy.

Wollstonecraft's challenge to traditional gender roles remains particularly relevant today. While significant strides have been made in achieving gender parity, many women still encounter societal expectations that hinder their full participation in various spheres. Wollstonecraft's advocacy for viewing women as equals—capable of rational thought and deserving of the same rights as men—is a reminder of the importance of dismantling entrenched biases and fostering inclusivity.

To truly honor Wollstonecraft's legacy, it is essential to apply her insights to the modern world. Education systems must continue evolving to ensure all individuals, irrespective of gender, can pursue their interests free from discrimination or limitation. Gender should never dictate one's opportunities or abilities; instead, merit and passion should guide personal and professional journeys.

Similarly, the relevance of her theories today lies in recognizing and addressing the multifaceted challenges women face globally. Intersectionality plays a crucial role in understanding how different identities—such as race, class, and sexual orientation—intersect with gender to shape unique experiences. By acknowledging these complexities, we can create more inclusive movements that advocate for justice and equality across diverse communities.

Wollstonecraft's vision was one of liberation—where women could achieve self-actualization without societal constraints. Her pioneering spirit serves as a source of inspiration for activists, educators, and leaders who strive to continue her work. Through collective efforts, society can move closer to realizing Wollstonecraft's dream of a world where women are empowered, respected, and valued for their contributions.

Wollstonecraft died on September 10, 1797, at the age of 38. She passed away shortly after giving birth to her second daughter, Mary, who would later become famous as the author of "Frankenstein." This context offers a glimpse into the challenges she faced as a woman and a mother during a time when women had limited rights and opportunities. The pressures of childbirth in the late 18th century were substantial, and many women did not survive the experience. Wollstonecraft's death highlights both the risks women faced in her era and her commitment to motherhood despite the societal constraints.

In terms of marital status, Wollstonecraft experienced significant ups and downs. She never married until later in her life. Her first significant relationship was with American businessman Gilbert Imlay, with whom she had her first child, Fanny. The two were never married, reflecting the complexities of relationships at that time, especially for women who desired independence. After a troubled relationship with Imlay, Wollstonecraft married the philosopher William Godwin in 1797. This marriage symbolized a blending of personal ideals with intellectual companionship.

Wollstonecraft had two children, Fanny and Mary. Fanny was born out of wedlock, a significant detail that showcases the limited social choices available to women. After her marriage to Godwin, Wollstonecraft gave birth to Mary, her second daughter. Her role as a mother deeply influenced her writing. She often expressed her thoughts on the importance of educating girls and women, believing that nurturing the mind was crucial for any mother.

The legacy of Mary Wollstonecraft extends beyond her immediate family and personal life. Her works challenged the status quo and encouraged others to think critically about gender roles and the position of women in society. In her book "A Vindication of the Rights of Woman," she argued that women should not be seen as mere ornaments to their husbands, but rather as fully capable individuals entitled to education and rights.

# Sojourner Truth's Impact on Women's Rights

Sojourner Truth (1797-1883) is another towering figure in the history of both the abolitionist and women's rights movements. Her activism powerfully influenced the concept of intersectionality, highlighting the connected struggles for freedom and equality.

Sojourner Truth was born in New York in 1797. Her birth name was Isabella Baumfree. She grew up in a time when slavery was a common practice in America. Truth was born into slavery, which meant that she was considered property instead of a person. She never knew her exact birthday, which is common for many people who were enslaved. As a child, she was separated from her family, as they were sold to different owners. This painful experience was a reality many enslaved children faced (*Sojourner Truth: Ain't I a Woman?*, 2017).

She worked on the farm, doing difficult tasks like plowing fields and caring for animals. Her owners were not kind, and she was treated poorly. Despite these challenges, she learned to be strong and resilient. She witnessed the struggles of her fellow slaves and understood the importance of fighting for freedom. This early exposure to the injustices of slavery shaped her beliefs and later influenced her activism.

Truth's early life was filled with hardship. At the age of nine, she was sold to another owner, who gave her the name Isabella. She faced numerous challenges under this new ownership. She was often beaten and treated with disrespect. During these years, Truth's spirit was tested, but she remained determined. She often dreamed of freedom, imagining a life where she could make her own choices and live without fear.

As she grew older, Truth's circumstances changed. She fell in love and had several children. Unfortunately, the laws of the time did not favor her, and her children were taken away from her multiple times. This was another heart-wrenching experience for the truth. She fought hard to keep her children safe and even managed to escape with one of them. This experience strengthened her passion to advocate for others who were suffering from similar injustices.

In 1826, Sojourner Truth made a significant decision. She escaped from slavery with the help of a friend. This moment marked the beginning of her journey toward freedom. Upon gaining her freedom, she changed her name to Sojourner Truth. This new name reflected her mission to travel and speak the truth about slavery and women's rights. She realized that sharing her story could help raise awareness and inspire change.

Truth faced many challenges as she began her speaking career. At first, people were skeptical of her because of her gender and background. However, she did not let this discourage her. She traveled from town to town, giving speeches about the struggles of the enslaved. Her eloquence and passion captured the attention of many. For instance, at a women's rights convention, she delivered her famous "Ain't I a Woman?" speech. In this speech, she powerfully addressed the double prejudice of being both Black and female, emphasizing that her strength and identity as a woman should not be undermined by her race (Michals, 2015).

Truth's speech resonated deeply with its audience due to her ability to articulate complex ideas about race and gender through simple yet compelling rhetoric. Her words dismantled stereotypes that denied women, particularly African American women, their agency and humanity. By asking repeatedly, "Ain't I a woman?" Truth urged listeners to recognize the full spectrum of womanhood beyond the white, middle-class standards typically upheld in society. This speech not only reinforced the call for women's suffrage but also insisted on equality across racial lines, making it a crucial pivot in feminist discourse (National Park Service, 2017).

Exploring Sojourner Truth's life reveals her as an enduring symbol of resilience and empowerment. Her personal journey—from enslavement to becoming a nationally recognized advocate—embodies extraordinary strength and determination. Truth's transformation into an itinerant preacher allowed her to connect with people from various backgrounds, mobilizing support for both abolitionist and women's rights causes. Her life story has been a source of inspiration for countless women facing adversity, symbolizing the possibility of overcoming seemingly insurmountable challenges (Walker, 2021).

The connection between abolition and feminism in Truth's work sheds light on the necessity of addressing multiple forms of oppression simultaneously. As a former slave who became involved in both movements, she understood that true liberation required comprehensive social change. Truth's approach revealed how the fight against slavery and the struggle for women's rights were inherently linked. By advocating for the rights of both African Americans and women, Truth demonstrated the importance of intersectional activism—a perspective acknowledging that individuals face layered discrimination based on race, gender, class, and more. This approach remains vital today as activists continue to combat pervasive inequalities across different spheres.

Modern activism still feels the impact of Sojourner Truth's contributions. Her legacy endures as a guiding force for today's social justice movements, reminding us that true equality requires embracing and supporting diversity within our struggles. Contemporary feminists draw inspiration from Truth's pioneering activism, integrating her principle of intersectionality into their advocacy efforts. Truth's insistence on visibility and voice for marginalized women continues to resonate, urging present-day leaders to address systemic injustices with the same fervor that motivated her campaigns. Her ability to speak truth to power has become a template for activists seeking to affect meaningful change across various fronts.

Sojourner Truth was married twice in her lifetime. Her first marriage was to a man named Thomas, who was also enslaved. However, it was difficult for them to maintain a family in the chaotic conditions of slavery. After her escape, she married again, but those details are less well documented. Despite her marital struggles, her identity as a mother is central to understanding her life journey.

Sojourner Truth's speeches are some of the most memorable parts of her legacy. She delivered powerful orations that spoke directly to the injustices faced by women and African Americans. Her most famous speech, "Ain't I a Woman?" is a direct challenge against the stereotypes and limitations placed on women, particularly black women. In her speeches, she often shared her personal story, which helped others relate to her message.

Truth passed away in 1883 at the age of 86. Her long life was filled with struggles and triumphs that not only impacted her but also resonated with many others. She witnessed several pivotal moments in American history, including the end of slavery and the early sparks of the women's rights movement.

Sojourner Truth's life reminds us of the struggles women, particularly black women, faced and continue to face. Her commitment to her cause did not waver, even in the face of adversity. By advocating for equal rights and using her voice to inspire those around her, she became a beacon of hope for many. Her story emphasizes the importance of resilience in the pursuit of justice.

In reviewing Sojourner Truth's life, it is essential to recognize not just her personal experiences but also the broader context of the times she lived in. The antebellum period was marked by stark divisions in society over issues of race and gender. Many women of her time were fighting for rights that we sometimes take for granted today.

The context of women's rights during her lifetime also plays a crucial role in understanding her significance. The Seneca Falls Convention in 1848 was a landmark event for the women's suffrage movement. Sojourner Truth's involvement in this movement placed her at the forefront of a crucial issue. Her tireless work for equality had a lasting impact that still resonates in the ongoing fight for social justice.

In addition to her work on women's rights, she was actively involved in the abolition movement. She traveled across the country, speaking at various events to raise awareness about the horrors of slavery. Her firsthand accounts as someone who experienced these injustices added credibility and urgency to her speeches. This dual focus on race and gender issues made her a unique and powerful figure in the civil rights movements of her time.

Sojourner Truth's challenging experiences shaped her views and actions. Her advocacy was not just personal; it was a reflection of a larger struggle for equality. Her story is a testament to the power of one individual to challenge the status quo and inspire change in society. Her legacy is preserved in both historical records and the ongoing discussions about race, gender, and justice.

By examining the lives of women who died young, one can also understand the broader societal conditions that often led to their early deaths. Sojourner Truth's life stands in stark contrast to many women of her time who did not have the same opportunities or access to rights. The struggles she faced were not solely personal; they were rooted in the systems of oppression that existed widely during her lifetime.

In conclusion, Sojourner Truth's life is a story of resilience, advocacy, and the relentless pursuit of justice. Her struggles, both as a mother and an activist, highlight the complexities of her identity and the challenges of her time. Understanding her experiences gives us deeper insight into the ongoing fight for equality that continues today.

# The Early Suffrage Movement Spearheaded by Susan B. Anthony

Susan B. Anthony (1820-1906) stands as a pillar of resilience and determination in the quest for women's suffrage, leaving an undeniable mark on both history and contemporary society. She tirelessly advocated for women's rights and equality throughout her life. She co-founded the National Woman Suffrage Association and was a key leader in the movement.

Susan was born on February 15, 1820, in Adams, Massachusetts. She was the second of eight children in a Quaker family that valued hard work and social justice. Growing up in a Quaker household significantly shaped her beliefs. Quakers believed in equality for all people, which influenced Anthony's views on women's rights and social reform (*Susan B. Anthony, icon of the women's suffrage movement,* 2019).

As a child, Susan was educated at home by her father, Daniel Anthony, who was a farmer and also a strong advocate for education. This education included reading, writing, and arithmetic, but she also learned about social issues and the importance of standing up for your beliefs. Susan showed an early interest in social justice, and the values taught by her family instilled in her a desire to fight for equality.

At the age of 15, she took a teaching job in a nearby school. This experience exposed her to the challenges faced by women in the workforce. She was paid less than her male counterparts, which angered her. But this first job experience had a lasting impact on her, and it sparked a fire in her to advocate for women's rights.

Her strategies learned throughout her life were valuable for the National Women's Studies Association (NWSA), as she used a blend of innovative organizing techniques and forged crucial alliances that propelled the crusade forward. The NWSA was formed to advocate for women's rights, particularly focusing on securing the right to vote. One can trace Anthony's strategic prowess back to her early days when she partnered with Elizabeth Cady Stanton, creating a dynamic duo that steered the NWSA through its formative years. Their collaboration was not just a meeting of minds but a fusion of complementary skills— Stanton with her intellectual rigor and Anthony with her organizational dexterity.

Together, they established the National Woman Suffrage Association (NWSA) in 1869, which became a central hub for feminist activism. The NWSA sought to secure voting rights for women through a constitutional amendment and served as a rallying point for activists nationwide. Anthony's leadership within this association was instrumental; she was known for her unwavering resolve and ability to galvanize support across different strata of society. Her role went beyond mere administration—she was a visionary who saw suffrage (the right to vote) not as an isolated cause but as a gateway to broader societal reforms designed to elevate women's roles and rights universally (GovInfo, 2019).

However, Anthony's journey was fraught with resistance. She encountered significant opposition from both individuals and institutions resistant to the idea of gender equality. Despite this, she persisted, exhibiting a resilience that would become the hallmark of her legacy. One notable instance of her fighting spirit occurred in 1872 when Anthony cast her vote in the presidential election—a bold assertion of her belief in women's right to vote despite legal prohibitions. Her subsequent arrest and trial highlighted the absurdity of denying voting rights based purely on gender, igniting public discourse and sympathy for the suffrage cause (Eisenberg & Ruthsdotter, 1998).

The challenges Anthony faced often intensified her resolve rather than diminished it. She understood the importance of public perception and utilized media coverage to further the movement's goals. Her speeches, travels, and relentless lobbying efforts kept women's suffrage at the forefront of national conversation, encouraging many women to join the fight for equal rights. In these endeavors, she worked closely with leaders such as Lucy Stone and Sojourner Truth, harnessing a collective strength that would prove decisive in overcoming societal obstacles.

Anthony's tireless advocacy laid a robust foundation for future advancements in women's rights. While she did not live to see the passage of the 19th Amendment in 1920, her influence was undeniable. This amendment, often referred to as the Susan B. Anthony Amendment, was the culmination of decades of steadfast activism, representing a triumph not only for Anthony but also for all those who had labored beside her during the struggle. Her life's work heralded a new era where women could aspire to participate fully in civic life, influencing laws and policies that impacted them directly (GovInfo, 2019).

Her legacy extends beyond the success of women's suffrage; it is enshrined in the broader pursuit of gender equality. Anthony's contributions have inspired successive generations of feminists and social activists, underscoring the principle that perseverance in the face of adversity can lead to transformative social change. Today, her life and work remain a testament to the power of dedicated activism, offering invaluable lessons to those continuing the fight for social justice and equality in various forms.

# Bringing It All Together

In this chapter, we explored the foundational ideas of feminism by delving into the lives and works of pioneering figures. We began with Mary Wollstonecraft, whose advocacy for women's education and autonomy laid the groundwork for future feminist movements. Her arguments illustrated the systemic nature of gender inequality, emphasizing the importance of dismantling artificial constructs that hindered women's progress. This journey continued with the influential voice of Sojourner Truth, whose iconic "Ain't I a Woman?" speech underscored the interconnected struggles of race and gender, challenging prevailing norms and advocating for comprehensive social change. Through these figures, we traced the evolution of feminism, highlighting its ongoing relevance as it addresses modern issues, such as wage gaps and underrepresentation in leadership roles.

This narrative not only reveals the enduring impact of early activists like Susan B. Anthony and Ada Lovelace, but also underscores the transformative power of their contributions to feminism and technology. Anthony's tireless campaign for women's suffrage demonstrated the strength of dedicated activism, while Lovelace's visionary work in computing broke societal stereotypes, paving the way for future innovations. By connecting these historical narratives, we gain insight into how past efforts continue to resonate and inspire contemporary movements for gender equality. As we reflect on these stories, it becomes evident that the fight for women's rights has been shaped by countless trailblazers whose legacies encourage us to continue advocating for justice and inclusivity across various spheres.

# Chapter 2:
# Pioneers of the Suffrage Movement

The pioneers of the suffrage movement significantly advanced women's rights by using a wide range of strategies to advocate for voting equality. Their relentless pursuit of justice and equal representation laid the groundwork for transformative social changes. This chapter discusses these influential actions and moments led by key figures within this movement. These women, through personal sacrifice and bold determination, challenged societal norms. By stepping into public advocacy, they opened doors for future generations to participate actively in democratic processes. In this chapter, we will discover the innovative tactics adopted by leaders like Emmeline Pankhurst, whose fearless approach redefined political activism.

# Emmeline Pankhurst's Militant Strategies and Success

Emmeline Pankhurst (1858-1928) was a significant leader in the British suffragette movement, known for her relentless fight for women's right to vote in the early 20th century. She employed bold and militant tactics to draw attention to the cause.

Emmeline was born on July 15, 1858, in Manchester, England. She came from a relatively well-off family, which helped shape her views on women's rights. Her parents, Robert and Sophia Pankhurst, were active in social issues, especially the fight against slavery. The dedication of her parents to social causes left a strong impression on Emmeline as a child. She saw how important social justice was to her family, and this influenced her future actions (Daniels, 2019).

From a young age, Emmeline was exposed to the idea that women could and should fight for their rights. She attended a school that encouraged her to think independently. This was not a typical education for girls at that time; most schools focused on homemaking skills, but Emmeline learned much more. For instance, she studied subjects such as history and mathematics. This education was crucial in developing her critical thinking skills. As a result, she became more aware of the inequalities that women faced in society.

Emmeline's upbringing also included her experiences with early activism. At the age of 14, she started participating in campaigns for social reform. This early involvement shaped her understanding of activism. For example, she joined her parents at meetings where they discussed issues like women's suffrage. These gatherings were not just events; they were passionate discussions about the rights of women and the injustices they faced. Watching her parents debate and argue for change fueled her desire to become actively involved in the fight for equality.

In 1879, Emmeline married Richard Pankhurst, a barrister who was also passionate about women's rights. Richard supported her ambitions and shared her beliefs about social justice. Their marriage was both a partnership and a commitment to fighting for the rights of women. Together, they attended various meetings and rallies. This partnership provided Emmeline with a strong foundation. She learned how to articulate her views and develop strategies for activism.

The couple had five children together, and while many women faced the challenge of balancing family life with activism, Emmeline took on the task with determination. She believed that her fight for women's rights was just as important as being a mother. This belief stems from her understanding that these rights would lead to a better world for her children. For example, after the birth of her children, Emmeline would bring them along to suffrage meetings, which helped to normalize activism in her family's life.

As Emmeline continued her journey, she became increasingly aware of the limitations placed on women. For instance, women were often denied the right to vote, to own property, or to have independence in their careers. These issues sparked a fire in her. Emmeline began organizing a women's suffrage group in Manchester. She wanted to create a community of like-minded women who could come together and demand their rights. The group focused on educating women about their rights and mobilizing them for campaigns.

Emmeline remarkable leadership in the suffrage movement was characterized by a fearless commitment to encourage change through direct action. Her formation of the Women's Social and Political Union (WSPU) marked a significant turning point in the fight for women's rights. Established in 1903, the WSPU arose from frustration at the inadequate progress being made through conventional methods. Pankhurst and her allies believed that more aggressive tactics were necessary to capture public attention and force legislative change. The motto "Deeds, not words" symbolized this radical shift in approach (Daniels, 2019).

Pankhurst's strategies involved bold and confrontational actions designed to disrupt societal norms and challenge the status quo. She led campaigns where members of the WSPU engaged in acts of civil disobedience, including protests, rallies, and public demonstrations, which were done with the intent to gain visibility for their cause. One notable event was the "rush" on Parliament in 1908, which drew thousands of participants eager to join the push for women's voting rights. These high-profile actions successfully spotlighted the movement and also led to consequential personal sacrifices, including imprisonment for many suffragettes.

Among the most prominent strategies practiced by the WSPU under Pankhurst's leadership were hunger strikes. These were not just acts of protest but also tools for showcasing the injustices faced by women fighting for equality. When imprisoned, many suffragettes, including Pankhurst herself, went on hunger strikes to draw attention to their plight and the brutality of their treatment. These strikes garnered sympathy from the public and displayed the determination and resilience of the women involved. Their sufferings forced society to confront the harsh realities of gender inequality, creating a wave of support that transcended social classes.

The impact of Emmeline Pankhurst's activism can be seen far beyond the immediate gains of the suffrage movement. Her legacy continues to resonate with modern movements advocating for gender equality. Pankhurst's fearless pursuit of justice and her innovative approaches to activism have inspired countless individuals and groups worldwide. Her influence is noticed through strategies used by current and recent campaigners who rely on similar principles of direct action and public engagement to effect social change. The lessons drawn from Pankhurst's life encourage today's activists to remain steadfast and creative in their efforts to advance women's rights.

Pankhurst's role within intersecting social movements also helped promote broader calls for justice. During World War I, she demonstrated her strategic awareness by aligning the fight for women's rights with the national war effort. Pankhurst believed that proving women's patriotism and competence would enhance their case for suffrage. While her stance was controversial, particularly among those who opposed the war, it strategically positioned women as indispensable to the nation's success. This alignment with larger societal goals highlighted Pankhurst's ability to adapt her strategies to evolving contexts, reinforcing the idea that the struggle for suffrage was part of a larger battle for equality and justice (Daniels, 2019).

Pankhurst also recognized the importance of coalitions across different social movements. Her understanding of the interconnectedness of various forms of discrimination and oppression improved her approach to advocacy. By engaging with labor movements and other reform groups, she amplified the message that women's rights were a crucial component of broader societal advancement. This approach emphasized the necessity of intersectionality in activism, a concept that remains vital in contemporary struggles for equality.

Emmeline Pankhurst's bold actions and strategic thinking significantly advanced the suffrage cause. The foundation of the WSPU marked a new era of direct action, capturing the public's imagination and generating widespread discussion about women's rights. Through tactics like hunger strikes, she brought light to systemic injustices and won crucial public empathy. Her legacy as a powerful figure in the suffrage movement continues to inspire modern activists who seek to achieve gender equality and social justice. Pankhurst's work has left an undeniable mark on the ongoing quest for women's rights and broader societal progress.

# Rosa Parks' Pivotal Role and Ripple Effect on Civil Rights

Rosa Parks (1913-2005) is an outstanding figure in the American civil rights movement, best known for her courageous act of refusing to give up her seat to a white passenger on a segregated bus in Montgomery, Alabama, in 1955. Her bold stand sparked the Montgomery Bus Boycott, becoming a pivotal event that galvanized efforts to end racial segregation and discrimination in the United States.

Rosa Parks was born on February 4, 1913, in Tuskegee, Alabama. She was raised in a time when racial discrimination and segregation were prevalent in the southern United States. Her childhood was marked by the realities of being an African American in a segregated society. Rosa's parents, James and Leona McCauley, separated when she was young. After the separation, Rosa and her mother moved to Pine Level, Alabama, to live with her grandparents. Growing up in a community where discrimination was common had a significant impact on her perspective on race and justice (Norwood, 2017).

Rosa Parks' upbringing was heavily influenced by her family. Her mother, Leona, worked as a teacher and instilled in Rosa the values of education and self-respect. Leona encouraged her to stand up for what was right. Rosa's grandfather was a significant figure in her life as well; he had been a hardworking man who shared stories about his experiences with racism. These family influences taught Rosa the importance of resilience. They showed her how to navigate a world filled with challenges (Norwood, 2017).

Education also influenced Rosa Parks' early life. She attended a segregated school, where resources were limited compared to schools for white students. Despite these challenges, Rosa excelled in her studies. She was passionate about learning and wanted a better future for herself and her community. One of the lessons she learned in school was the importance of fighting against injustice. Even as a young girl, Rosa understood that education was a tool for empowerment. She participated in various school activities, which further developed her passion for civil rights.

The segregation laws in Alabama greatly affected Parks' upbringing. She witnessed firsthand the inequalities faced by her community. For instance, African Americans had to sit at the back of the bus and were often treated with disrespect. These experiences left a lasting impression on Rosa, making her determined to challenge the status quo. She realized that staying silent would not bring about change. Rosa's observations of segregation created within her a strong desire to fight for justice. This foundation of resilience would later influence her actions as an activist.

Rosa Parks' act of defiance on December 1, 1955 (at the age of 43) marked a crucial turning point in the struggle for racial and gender equality. On that day, Parks refused to relinquish her seat to a white man on a Montgomery, Alabama bus, sparking what would become the historic Montgomery Bus Boycott (History.com Editors, 2009). This courageous decision demonstrated the profound impact one can have in igniting collective action. At that time, public buses in the U.S. had separate areas and designed seats for white people and people of color. The boycott, which lasted over a year, emerged as a powerful demonstration of solidarity within the Black community, significantly altering the course of the civil rights movement.

Parks' refusal was not a spontaneous gesture, but a carefully considered statement against entrenched injustice. At the time, she served as the secretary of the youth division at the local NAACP chapter and had been actively involved in civil rights activism. Her determination stemmed from witnessing numerous injustices, including the recent discharge of Emmett Till's murderers. This event fueled her commitment to resisting oppression and highlighted how deeply intertwined the fights for racial and gender equality were. Her act showcased the power of peaceful protest in challenging systemic discrimination and inspired others to join the fight for justice (NAACP, 2022).

The influence of Parks extended far beyond the confines of the Montgomery buses. Her dedication to the movement became a symbol of resistance against both racial and gender-based discrimination, illustrating the interconnectedness of these struggles. While the primary focus of her actions appeared to be aimed at racial segregation, they also signaled a broader challenge to the societal norms that degraded women to subordinate roles. Parks'role in the civil rights movement encouraged women to take on more active roles in advocacy, demonstrating that their voices were vital in shaping equitable futures.

Following the success of the Montgomery Bus Boycott, Parks continued to advocate for the cause of equality through her work in various movements. After relocating to Detroit, she worked with Congressman John Conyers Jr., where she lent her efforts to address issues like job discrimination and affordable housing (History.com Editors, 2009). Her commitment to empowering women and fighting for social justice persisted well into her later years. Through her co-founding of the Rosa and Raymond Parks Institute for Self-Development, Parks provided educational programs for young people, particularly focusing on underserved communities. Her work exemplified how activism could evolve while maintaining its foundational goals of equality and justice.

Parks also symbolized hope and resilience despite constant adversity. Facing personal repercussions—such as losing her job and enduring harassment—did not deter her spirit. Instead, these challenges encouraged her to become yet another testament to her role as a lasting icon of defiance and strength. Parks' journey emphasizes the importance of perseverance in the face of overwhelming opposition and serves as a beacon of motivation for future generations fighting against oppression.

Her legacy is a reminder of the critical role each one of us plays in challenging and dismantling oppressive systems. Through her singular refusal to give in, Parks mobilized an entire community, setting off a chain of events that would forever alter the trajectory of civil rights in America. The Montgomery Bus Boycott became a blueprint for non-violent protest, inspiring movements across the globe seeking similar change and equality.

Rosa Parks' life work also stresses the importance of solidarity within movements for societal change. By interlinking her fight for racial and gender equality, she demonstrated the necessity for inclusive approaches to addressing social injustices. Her involvement in both spheres shows that progress can only be achieved when all voices, particularly those historically marginalized, are uplifted and heard. Park's role as a unifying figure in these overlapping struggles highlights the need for collaborative efforts in the pursuit of true equality.

The resonance of Parks' actions continues to inspire new generations of activists dedicated to advocating for justice and equality. Her story provides a powerful narrative that encourages us all to recognize our potential impact, regardless of the scale of our actions. As we reflect on her contributions, it becomes evident that social movements often hinge on the bravery of one person willing to challenge the status quo and inspire others to envision a fairer world.

In celebrating Parks as an enduring symbol of resistance, it is essential to acknowledge her multifaceted contributions to the advancement of both racial and gender equality. Her legacy is not confined to a single moment of defiance, but rather encompasses a lifetime of dedication to justice and empowerment. Parks remains a guiding light, illuminating the path forward for those committed to building inclusive societies free from oppression.

# Impact of the 19th Amendment in the United States

The authorization of the 19th Amendment in 1920 was a landmark achievement in American history, symbolizing a hard-fought victory for women's voting rights. This amendment came about from decades of unyielding struggle by countless women who dedicated their lives to the cause of suffrage. From the mid-19th century onwards, these advocates relentlessly lectured, wrote, marched, and lobbied to alter what many perceived as the deeply entrenched gender norms of their time. The passage of this pivotal legislation granted American women the legal right to vote and also announced a new era of potential participation in democratic processes. The journey from proposal to authorization was strenuous. It was marked by diverse strategies ranging from state-level campaigns to radical acts of civil disobedience, as activists encountered fierce resistance and continuously persevered in their mission (*19th Amendment to the U.S. Constitution: Women's Right to Vote (1920)*, 2022).

Despite the monumental passage of the 19th Amendment, its implementation highlighted enduring injustice in access to voting rights. While the amendment was a triumph of legal recognition, many women, particularly those from marginalized communities, still faced formidable barriers. Discriminatory state laws, especially in the Southern states, continued to oppress African American women, Native American women, Asian American women, and other minority groups. These obstacles persisted well into the 20th century until they were gradually dismantled through further legislative efforts, such as the Voting Rights Act of 1965 (*Impact of the Nineteenth Amendment beyond the Supreme Court | Constitution Annotated | Congress.gov | Library of Congress*, 2020). While the 19th Amendment marked a significant step forward, it didn't end the ongoing struggle for full electoral inclusion.

In addition to its immediate impacts, the 19th Amendment served as a catalyst for broader social change and inspired subsequent movements representing gender equality. It signified legal victory and a notable cultural shift, empowering women across the nation to pursue greater political involvement and representation. This empowerment laid the groundwork for the feminist movements of the 1960s and beyond, as women began advocating for voting rights and equal opportunities in education, employment, and leadership roles within society. The achievements catalyzed by the 19th Amendment show us that securing one fundamental right can open the doors to broader dialogues and demands for justice.

Furthermore, the success of the 19th Amendment reached far beyond the United States, influencing global suffrage movements and emphasizing the significance of international solidarity among activists. Women around the world found inspiration in this success, recognizing that unified efforts could lead to substantial societal change. The cross-pollination of ideas and tactics among international suffragists strengthened global networks and led to similar reforms in other countries.

# Influence of Global Suffrage Movements on Local Actions

In the worldwide struggle for women's suffrage, diverse international movements offer a rich knowledge of shared experiences, strategies, and aspirations that crossed borders and transformed local campaigns. These global influences helped to shape the suffrage movement as an interconnected network of activists, drawing strength and inspiration from each other's victories and challenges.

The emergence of international suffrage efforts during the late 19th and early 20th centuries inspired an unprecedented level of collaboration among activists worldwide. Women leaders recognized that while their immediate challenges might differ, they were united by the common goal of securing voting rights. Organizations such as the International Council of Women (founded in 1888) and the International Women Suffrage Alliance (established in 1904) helped to create platforms for women to exchange ideas and develop unified strategies across national boundaries. These organizations facilitated international conferences and publications, enabling dialogue among activists from various countries. Such interactions allowed women to share successful tactics and adapt them to their unique cultural and political landscapes (Ware, 2020).

These international exchanges encouraged activists to learn from one another's successes and setbacks. For instance, suffragists in New Zealand and Australia achieved early legislative victories, granting women the right to vote in 1893 and 1902, respectively. Their accomplishments provided crucial lessons for suffrage campaigns in other parts of the world. American and British suffragists eagerly studied these examples, understanding that both strategic patience and persistence could eventually result in victory. The transference of knowledge did not merely involve copying successful models, but also entailed adapting them to local contexts, recognizing that cultural nuances and political systems varied significantly from one country to another. This adaptability was vital in creating unique and specified approaches that resonated with local populations and governments alike (Marino, 2019).

Examining the roles of global leaders alongside domestic figures offers a more comprehensive view of suffrage movements. While iconic figures like Susan B. Anthony and Elizabeth Cady Stanton are often highlighted, it is essential to acknowledge the contributions of non-Western leaders who enriched the movement's diversity. Latin American feminists such as Bertha Lutz played influential roles in advocating for women's rights through international forums, including the creation of the United Nations Commission on the Status of Women in 1945. These leaders were instrumental in ensuring that women's rights were included in emerging global human rights agendas, setting precedents for later feminist advocacy around the world. Their activism demonstrated that the quest for suffrage was not confined to any single region, but was indeed a universal pursuit (Ware, 2020).

In Iceland, women had been advocating and fighting for women's right to vote since 1885 and on June 19. 1915 a law was passed giving women the right to vote and to run for parliament (Iceland Women's History Museum, 2020). However, they were required to have turned 40 to have the suitable maturity to vote, sending a false message to women that they were behind men in maturity.

Moreover, global organizations helped to support and promote women's rights initiatives. The International Women Suffrage Alliance, for example, committed itself to securing the enfranchisement of women globally. It served as a beacon of hope for countless women who lacked the resources or networks to embark on solo campaigns. By uniting marginal groups under a common cause, these organizations lent credibility and weight to suffrage demands, forcing governments to take notice. They provided financial support, organized rallies, and lobbied international bodies to pressure reluctant nations into reforming their electoral laws. The impact of these organizations helped to nurture a sense of unity and purpose among women fighting for their rights, regardless of geographical location (Marino, 2019).

These global efforts illustrate how collaborative action can transcend borders, providing valuable resources and insights to bolster domestic movements. By examining the international dimension of the suffrage movement, we gain a fuller understanding of its complexities and the myriad forces that shaped its trajectory. Today, the legacy of these pioneers serves as a powerful reminder that the fight for gender equality cannot be waged in isolation but requires collective effort and unwavering resolve.

# Concluding Thoughts

In this chapter, we discussed the taxing battle for women's voting rights, highlighting the significant figures and events that have sculpted women's political landscape. Emmeline Pankhurst's fearless leadership and strategic tactics had a tremendous influence on the suffrage movement, showing us how resilient activism could challenge and change societal norms. Her approach of "Deeds not words" catalyzed a more dynamic phase of activism, resonating deeply with those striving for gender equality. Similarly, Rosa Parks' bold act of defiance became a pivotal force in the civil rights movement, illustrating each person's role in collective action. Her intertwined fight against both racial and gender injustice depicted the essential connection between these struggles, inspiring women to take active parts in advocacy.

The authorization of the 19th Amendment marked a historic victory, granting American women the right to vote and setting the stage for future efforts toward gender equality. The ongoing influence of global suffrage movements underscored the interconnectedness of these campaigns, enabling activists worldwide to share strategies and support each other's missions. By engaging with international networks, women gained valuable insights that strengthened their local efforts while contributing to broader societal changes. The stories of these leaders provide inspiration and guidance for today's activists, encouraging a commitment to justice and a reminder that progress relies on solidarity and perseverance among those fighting for equal rights. Now that we've discussed the women of the suffrage movement, we can move on to some women in STEM who broke barriers in male-dominated industries.

# Chapter 3:
# Breaking Barriers: Women in Science and Technology

Breaking barriers in science and technology has been a challenging journey for women, driven by their passion and intellectual expertise. These influential women defied societal norms and set the stage for future generations to explore science and innovation without limitations. In this chapter, we will discuss the inspiring stories of prominent female figures who have made significant contributions to science and technology, showcasing their achievements and the lasting impact they've had on these fields. Examining their journeys reveals the milestones they achieved and the personal and systemic challenges they overcame. This chapter celebrates both individual accomplishments and collective progress within the realms of science and technology.

# Ada Lovelace's Foundational Work in Computing

Augusta Ada King (1815-1852), Countess of Lovelace, known today as Ada Lovelace, was a visionary mathematician whose work with Charles Babbage (1791-1871) on the Analytical Engine marked a key turning point in the history of computing. At a time when women's contributions to science and technology were largely undervalued, her insights laid the foundational stone for modern computing, earning her recognition as the world's first computer programmer.

Augusta Ada King, known as Ada Lovelace, was born in London on December 10, 1815. She came from a well-known family. Her father was the famous poet Lord Byron, and her mother, Annabella Milbanke, was a mathematician. Their backgrounds played a significant role in Ada's life. Even though her father left when she was very young, Ada's mother made sure that she had a strict education, especially in mathematics and science. This decision had a lasting impact on Ada's future (The Editors of Encyclopaedia Britannica, 2018).

Ada grew up in an environment that encouraged her to think logically. Her mother believed that if Ada studied math and science, she would avoid the emotional tendencies of her father. Annabella often arranged for her daughter to meet several prominent mathematicians and scientists of the time. These meetings inspired Ada and helped her develop a love for numbers and calculations. Her early exposure to logical thought laid the groundwork for her future achievements.

During her childhood, Ada was very curious and inquisitive. She enjoyed asking questions and seeking answers. For example, she once asked her mother about steam power and how it worked. This curiosity led to her creating complex projects, including designing a flying machine. Ada often traveled with her mother to various places that further enriched her understanding of the world around her. These experiences provided her with unique insights that shaped her innovative thinking.

When Ada was around ten years old, her education became more structured. Her mother hired tutors to help her learn complicated subjects. One of her tutors was the mathematician Mary Somerville, who introduced Ada to many scientific ideas. Somerville's guidance played an essential role in Ada's academic journey, showing her the works of prominent scientists and mathematicians. Under their guidance, Ada developed a strong understanding of mathematics, which would later help her work on computer programming.

As Ada grew older, her interests expanded beyond mathematics. She became fascinated with the emerging field of computing. At the age of seventeen, she met Charles Babbage, who would later become a significant influence in her life. Babbage was working on his Analytical Engine, an early mechanical computer. Ada's keen interest in Babbage's work led her to collaborate with him. This partnership allowed her to explore her potential and pursue her passions more seriously.

Lovelace's partnership with Charles Babbage began when she was introduced to him in 1833 through mutual acquaintances. Babbage was already renowned for his ambitious projects, particularly the Difference Engine, designed to automate complex calculations (The Editors of Encyclopaedia Britannica, 2018). However, it was his next endeavor, the Analytical Engine, which captured Lovelace's imagination and became the focus of her most significant contributions. The Analytical Engine is often considered a conceptual precursor to the modern computer due to its ability to perform arithmetic tasks and even more complex operations—a fact recognized by Lovelace long before her contemporaries.

What set Ada Lovelace apart from others who worked with Babbage was her deep understanding of the potential of such machines. In 1843, when translating an article written by Luigi Federico Menabrea on the Analytical Engine, Lovelace went beyond mere translation. Her annotations expanded upon Babbage's design speculations with remarkable foresight, articulating ideas that machines could handle symbols as well as numbers. This was a revolutionary notion at the time because it proposed that machines might one day process information and instructions symbolically, a concept practiced today by modern computing (Siffert, 2024).

Perhaps the most groundbreaking of Lovelace's contributions is encapsulated in what she termed Note G, where she outlined an algorithm intended to be executed by the Analytical Engine. This was essentially the first computer program, even though this machine was never built in her lifetime. The algorithm she devised for computing Bernoulli numbers demonstrated mathematical skills along with her ability to foresee computers' creative potential. Her work identified the need for systematic programming languages, recognizing that computation could extend into realms of art and music, catalyzing creativity rather than just performing automated tasks (The Editors of Encyclopaedia Britannica, 2018).

Lovelace's conceptualization of software was decades ahead of her time. While many saw Babbage's machine as a glorified calculator, Ada imagined a future whereby these engines could execute complex sequences of operations far beyond basic arithmetic. She envisioned machines capable of creating artwork or composing music by handling symbolic data, laying the groundwork for what we now understand as software engineering.

Her remarkable predictions about the capabilities of computing machines have echoed into modern times, influencing subsequent generations of computer scientists and innovators. Despite living in a society where her scientific talents were curtailed by patriarchal norms, Lovelace's work has surpassed those limitations, shining brightly in the records of history (The Editors of Encyclopaedia Britannica, 2018).

Ada Lovelace's life offers a powerful narrative of perseverance and intellectual courage. Her contributions are particularly inspiring given the challenges she faced, as women in the 19th century struggled against societal norms that restricted their educational opportunities and scientific pursuits. Born into privilege yet constrained by the very gender norms that aimed to limit her, Lovelace leveraged her background and education to collaborate with leading scientists and contribute meaningfully to technological progress.

The legacy of Ada Lovelace serves as a beacon of hope and inspiration for women today, especially those keenly interested in the fields of science, technology, engineering, and mathematics (STEM). She exemplifies how a dedicated vision and intellectual curiosity can transcend societal limitations and pave the way for groundbreaking innovations in history. Ada Lovelace Day, celebrated every second Tuesday in October, continues to honor her achievements and encourage women globally to pursue STEM fields without fear of societal constraints (Siffert, 2024).

# Marie Curie's Dual Nobel Recognition and Its Implications

Marie Curie's (1867-1934) journey into the world of science marks one of the most compelling stories in the history of feminism and scientific achievement. Her life story is not just about groundbreaking discoveries, but also about breaking societal norms and redefining women's roles in science.

Marie Curie was born in Warsaw, Poland, in 1867. She was the youngest of five children in a family that valued education. Her father was a math and physics teacher, and her mother was a school director. This educational environment significantly influenced Marie's early years. She grew up in a culture that emphasized knowledge and curiosity. From a young age, Curie showed a keen interest in science and mathematics. She would often spend hours exploring the physics tools her father used in his classes. This early exposure sparked her interest in pursuing a career in science (*Marie Curie's Achievements*, n.d.).

However, in late 19th century Europe, women faced significant barriers when it came to education. Many universities did not allow women to enroll. In Poland, at the time, the opportunities for higher education were exceedingly limited for girls. Despite these obstacles, Marie was determined to learn. She participated in a secret educational program known as the "Flying University." This underground initiative offered women the chance to study subjects that were not available to them in public institutions. Through this program, Marie acquired knowledge in math and physics, laying important groundwork for her future studies.

Marie's family faced financial difficulties after the death of her mother when Marie was just ten years old. This loss impacted her deeply, also changing the dynamics within the family. Marie had to take on more responsibilities at a young age. Despite these challenges, she didn't lose sight of her educational goals. She worked hard to help support her siblings while still pursuing her studies. This determination influenced her resilience and commitment to her education, traits that would later define her career.

After completing her secondary education, Marie was eager to attend university. However, she faced the usual hurdles. Women were simply not accepted in many universities. Realizing that she might have to leave her home country to pursue her aspirations, she made a bold choice. At the age of 24, she moved to Paris to continue her studies at the Sorbonne. The move was daunting. She left behind her family and everything she knew, but she was motivated by the chance to learn in an environment where women had more opportunities.

Once in Paris, life was not easy for Marie. She encountered the challenges of adapting to a new culture and language. She lived in poverty, often struggling to afford basic necessities. Despite these hardships, she excelled in her studies. Marie was driven by a passion for science and a desire to make a name for herself in a male-dominated field. She embraced the demanding academic life at the Sorbonne. She studied physics and mathematics, and her dedication paid off.

As she settled into life in Paris, Marie discovered the work of other scientists. She was particularly influenced by the research being conducted on radioactivity. This area of study captivated her. It combined her interests in physics with a hands-on approach to experimentation. She began collaborating with other scientists, which helped her gain valuable experience in the laboratory. This exposure not only enhanced her knowledge but also built her confidence as a scientist (*Marie Curie's Achievements*, n.d.).

Marie met Pierre Curie in Paris while she was conducting her research. At the time, she was a Polish immigrant studying at the University of Paris. Pierre was a well-respected physicist known for his work in magnetism. Their initial connection was based on their shared passion for science. Marie was drawn to Pierre's intellect and dedication to his work. As they spent more time together, their relationship developed. They found common ground in their love for research and discovery. This bond grew deeper, leading them to marry in 1895. Their wedding was modest, reflecting their personalities and priorities. Marie Curie's marriage determination to prove herself continued to drive her forward. She worked tirelessly, often spending countless hours in the lab. The environment was challenging, but Marie's work ethic never wavered. She often reminisced about her childhood struggles and the barriers she faced. These memories fueled her ambition to succeed. As she delved deeper into her research, she began to make significant contributions to the understanding of radioactivity. Her work was slowly gaining recognition, though she still faced skepticism from some in the scientific community.

One of Curie's most storied achievements was becoming the first woman to win a Nobel Prize. In 1903, she shared the Nobel Prize in Physics with her husband and Henri Becquerel for their collective work on radioactivity. This recognition was monumental, marking her extraordinary capability in a field dominated by men and also setting a precedent for future generations of women. By breaking through this barrier, Curie demonstrated that gender should not define one's ability to excel in scientific pursuits. Women across the globe were inspired by this message and achievement, helping them to realize new potential within themselves to dream beyond traditional constraints.

Curie's pioneering research introduced the world to the phenomena of radioactivity. She coined the term itself, delving deeply into the mysterious emissions from certain materials. Through meticulous experimentation and research, Curie discovered two new elements: polonium, named after her homeland, and radium. These monumental contributions had far-reaching implications, transforming the medical world and leading to new treatments, including cancer therapies. As a result, Curie's work laid the foundation for modern radiology and advanced diagnostics, showcasing how science and research can massively impact society.

The recognition of Curie's second Nobel Prize in Chemistry in 1911 emphasized the significance of her contributions. She remains the only individual to receive Nobel Prizes in two different sciences, a testament to her relentless pursuit of knowledge and excellence despite significant obstacles. Her achievements demolished prevalent misconceptions about women's intellectual capabilities, inspiring countless young women to pursue careers in science (*Marie Curie*, n.d.).

Despite her scientific acclaim, Marie Curie faced pervasive gender-based discrimination throughout her career. The French Academy of Sciences refused her membership solely because of her gender, a stark reminder of the societal barriers she continuously confronted. When presenting their work, Pierre was often chosen to speak because women were not permitted to give lectures. Yet Curie never allowed these hindrances to impede her progress. Her resilience in the face of adversity serves as a powerful example for all women striving to overcome challenges imposed by a male-dominated society.

Amid these challenges, Curie took steps to institutionalize scientific research. After being appointed as the first woman faculty member at the University of Paris, she founded the Radium Institute, a beacon for scientific advancement and collaboration. On 4 July 1934, at the Sancellemoz Sanatorium in Passy, France, at the age of 66, Marie Curie died. The cause of her death was given as aplastic pernicious anemia, a condition she developed after years of exposure to radiation through her work (*Marie Curie the Scientist*, 2016). This institution, later renamed the Curie Institute, became pivotal in developing a new generation of scientists, including women who were motivated by Curie's unyielding spirit and accomplishments.

Her legacy continued through her daughter, Irène Joliot-Curie, who followed in her footsteps by winning a Nobel Prize in chemistry. This familial continuity highlights Curie's influence in both her immediate surroundings and extending to the broader scientific community. It shows us how one powerful figure can set off a chain reaction, inspiring others to contribute significantly to the fields they love.

In addition to her scientific endeavors, during World War I, Curie developed mobile X-ray units, which she personally took to the front lines. These "petite Curies" proved invaluable, enabling battlefield surgeries and saving countless soldiers' lives. Her commitment to practical applications of scientific principles further endeared her to society while granting her respect beyond academic circles, illustrating a broader impact through humanitarian efforts (*Marie Curie*, n.d.).

Marie Curie's story resonates across generations, offering hope and a blueprint for overcoming societal limitations. Her life emphasizes the necessity of breaking barriers in the pursuit of knowledge, advocating for gender equality, and embracing the diverse talents of individuals irrespective of their background. Curie's narrative is historic and deeply motivational, urging us to envision a future where everyone is afforded equal opportunity to contribute to society through science and innovation. Her legacy continues to guide discussions on women's rights and social justice, providing fertile ground for educators and activists to engage communities regarding the critical role of gender equality in shaping a more equitable world.

# Contributions of Hedy Lamarr to Modern Communication

Hedy Lamarr's (1914-2000) story is a powerful testament to the often-overlooked contributions of women in science and technology. She is an interesting figure not only for her successful career as a Hollywood actress during the Golden Age of Cinema but also for her groundbreaking contributions to technology

Hedy Lamarr was born in Vienna, Austria, in 1914 and grew up in a rich cultural environment that encouraged her artistic inclinations, thanks to her pianist mother and successful businessman father. This supportive backdrop significantly nurtured her creative abilities.

From a young age, Hedy displayed extraordinary curiosity and intelligence, showing an interest in science and technology. She often engaged with gadgets and was influenced by contemporary scientific advancements, which would later impact her innovative career. At 16, she began acting in Vienna, quickly gaining recognition for her beauty and talent. Her role in the controversial film "Ecstasy" in 1933 set the stage for her rise in the film industry. Despite the pressures of fame, she remained dedicated to her dual passions for acting and technology.

Relocating to Hollywood before World War II transformed her life, and she became one of its most glamorous stars. Her magnetic performances captivated audiences, but her intellect drove her to use her influence to explore scientific endeavors. Throughout her Hollywood career, Lamarr sought knowledge in technology, participating in discussions with inventors and engineers. She became involved in communication technology during World War II,, learning the science behind it and collaborating with composer George Antheil to co-create frequency-hopping spread spectrum technology—an innovation that enhanced secure radio communications.

This groundbreaking invention paved the way for advancements in mobile and wireless communications, though her contributions went unrecognized for many years. Many in the scientific community dismissed her due to her Hollywood image, showcasing the ongoing challenges for women in male-dominated spaces.

Despite facing numerous obstacles, Lamarr advocated for her invention to military officials during World War II, proposing its application for torpedo guidance. Although initially overlooked, her work is now acknowledged as a crucial foundation for modern communication technology.

Lamarr's inspiration for this invention came from a desire to aid the Allied forces during WWII. At the time, radio-controlled torpedoes were vulnerable to enemy jamming, which could lead to catastrophic failures. Lamarr and Antheil tackled this problem by creating a system where the transmitter and receiver would hop between frequencies in unison, making it nearly impossible for enemies to intercept or disrupt the signals. This innovative approach was secured with U.S. Patent No. 2,292,387 in 1942. Unfortunately, the U.S. Navy initially dismissed the technology, not recognizing its potential until decades later. Despite this initial setback, Lamarr's work has had lasting implications for military communications, underscoring that intellect and innovation can transcend traditional gender roles, especially in life-changing historical contexts (*Hedy Lamarr*, n.d.).

Though Lamarr's contributions went largely unrecognized during her lifetime, her posthumous recognition has sparked essential conversations about acknowledging women's roles in technological advancements. In 1997, she was belatedly honored by the Electronic Frontier Foundation with a Pioneer Award, and in 2014, 14 years after her death, she was inducted into the National Inventors Hall of Fame. These honors highlight a broader societal need to re-evaluate and celebrate the contributions of women whose work may have been undervalued or ignored. Recognizing Lamarr's achievements corrects historical oversight and encourages a more inclusive view of technology and innovation.

Another layer to Hedy Lamarr's legacy is her career as both a film star and an inventor. Balancing two distinct yet successful careers showcases the multifaceted talents women possess and the vast potential they can harness when given the opportunity. Her dual career serves as an inspiring example for women who aspire to pursue diverse paths and break away from conventional career expectations. Lamarr's life encourages exploration beyond set boundaries, illustrating that women's capabilities and interests are as varied and expansive as those of men.

A significant takeaway from Lamarr's narrative is the power of storytelling in shaping perceptions and inspiring future generations. By revisiting and elevating her accomplishments, society can challenge the narratives that have historically marginalized women's contributions. Acknowledging her work sparks important discussions that create spaces where women in tech can be seen, heard, and celebrated, thereby reinforcing the idea that success is not restricted by gender.

# Advancement of Female Participation in Scientific Discoveries

Throughout history, the role of women in science and technology has evolved significantly, reflecting broader societal changes toward greater inclusivity. Educational advancements have been pivotal in enhancing women's participation in these fields as more women gain access to higher education and professional opportunities. This shift shows us how we can systematically dismantle barriers that previously hindered women's advancement.

Historically, women faced numerous challenges in accessing quality education, particularly in fields like science and technology. Early pioneers, such as Rear Admiral Grace Murray Hopper, broke through these barriers by contributing significantly to computer programming language development (the White House, 2015). Their work laid the foundation for generations of women who continue to break new ground in scientific research and technological innovation. Katherine Johnson's critical calculations during the Space Race—a testament to her profound expertise and determination—are an example of how educational opportunities can lead to groundbreaking achievements (NASA, 2015).

Educational institutions today have become more inclusive, offering programs and scholarships specifically aimed at encouraging women to enter STEM fields. The success of Maria Klawe, the first female president of Harvey Mudd College, demonstrates the important role educational leaders play in fostering a more equal environment. Under her leadership, the percentage of women majoring in computer science at the college increased significantly, providing a model for other institutions seeking to achieve similar goals (MAKERS, 2015).

Women's scientific societies have played an instrumental role in supporting women's endeavors in male-dominated fields. These societies, which provide crucial networking and mentorship opportunities, help combat the isolation that many women face in such environments. By connecting female scientists with mentors and peers, these societies empower women to navigate challenges and share their experiences. For instance, initiatives like the Grace Hopper Celebration provide platforms for networking and learning, celebrating women's contributions to computing while fostering community and collaboration (U.S. Navy, 2015).

Contemporary female leaders continually challenge prevailing norms, breaking down barriers for future generations. Figures like Lydia Villa-Komaroff, a trailblazer in molecular biology, faced substantial opposition yet persevered, demonstrating resilience and the importance of supporting diversity within scientific communities (Thomas, 2022). Their success stories offer blueprints for young women aspiring to similar careers, illustrating how persistence and collaboration can pave new pathways in science.

The growing presence of women in science and technology helps reshape societal narratives about scientific accomplishments. As more women participate in and contribute to scientific discoveries and innovations, public perceptions evolve, redefining traditional views on gender roles in these sectors. Rachel Carson's environmental advocacy is a prime example of how one woman's efforts initiated a broader movement, changing how society views environmental responsibility and activism (U.S. Fish and Wildlife Service, 2015).

As these narratives continue to shift, it becomes clear that expanding opportunities for women in science benefits society as a whole. When women are included equitably in scientific research and technological development, diverse perspectives contribute to more robust and innovative solutions to complex problems. Encouragingly, this expansion also inspires young girls to envision themselves as future scientists and innovators.

To further encourage the inclusion of women in science and technology, guidelines and support systems are essential. Educational policies should continue focusing on making STEM fields accessible and appealing to women from diverse backgrounds. Additionally, expanding the reach and influence of women's scientific societies can provide the necessary mentorship and resources to nurture emerging talent. Leaders within these fields must remain committed to advocating for gender equality, ensuring that future generations inherit a fair and welcoming environment.

# Summary and Reflections

This chapter unearthed the transformative contributions of women in science and technology, emphasizing their enduring impact. Ada Lovelace's groundbreaking work laid the foundation for computing, envisioning machines as more than just calculators but as creative tools capable of symbolic processing. Her foresight into the potential of computing continues to inspire future generations. Similarly, Marie Curie's pioneering research in radioactivity redefined women's roles in science, earning her dual Nobel Prizes and influencing countless young women to pursue scientific careers despite societal constraints. Her resilience in the face of discrimination reminds us of the importance of perseverance and determination in achieving excellence.

The chapter also followed the story of Hedy Lamarr's inventive genius, which, though initially overlooked, established the basis for modern communication technologies like Wi-Fi. Her story demonstrates that innovation transcends traditional gender roles and highlights the necessity of recognizing women's contributions. Through these inspiring stories, we can learn that these powerful and intellectual women paved the way for us today. Although these spaces in STEM are still male-dominated, we have a voice and can explore great opportunities in these fields, irrespective of gender.

# Chapter 4:
# Women in Leadership: Political Transformations

Women in leadership have been pivotal in expanding the horizons of political landscapes globally. Their journeys are both personal triumphs and narrative arcs that redefine the power dynamics within traditionally male-dominated arenas. As we dive into the lives and influences of women like Indira Gandhi, Angela Merkel, Julia Gillard, and Tsai Ing-wen, we can reveal threads of courage and resilience woven through each story. These women have broken barriers, proving that gender does not limit our capacity to lead effectively. Their ascensions to power showcase their resolve to challenge societal norms and present a model for women worldwide who envision themselves in roles of influence. This chapter explores these transformative journeys, shedding light on how these women navigated unique challenges and left an important mark on their respective nations.

# Indira Gandhi's Influence as India's First Female Prime Minister

Indira Gandhi (1917-1984) is a remarkable figure as the first and only female Prime Minister of India, known for her strong leadership during a transformative period in the country's history and her efforts to implement significant social and economic reforms.

Indira Gandhi was born on November 19, 1917, in Allahabad, India. She was the only child of Jawaharlal Nehru and Kamala Nehru. From her early years, Indira lived in a politically active household. Her father, Jawaharlal Nehru, would later become India's first Prime Minister. This environment surrounded her with discussions about freedom, politics, and social issues. The optimism and determination of her parents greatly influenced her views and ambitions (The Editors of Encyclopedia Britannica, 2019).

Unfortunately, as a child, Indira faced health challenges. She was often sick and spent a lot of time at home. Her parents made sure that she received a good education during these times, and they provided her with a good and safe home. She studied various subjects, gaining knowledge in history, literature, and geography. The family valued education, and this helped shape Indira's understanding of the world. Later on, her health improved, and she was able to attend school more regularly.

Indira's early education involved attending the well-known schools in Allahabad. She was a bright student and showed a keen interest in learning. The encouragement from her parents' encouragement her to pursue her studies. As she grew older, her education continued abroad. She attended the prestigious Visva-Bharati University in Santiniketan, founded by Rabindranath Tagore. Here, she learned about culture and arts, further shaping her personality.

Indira's time in Europe was significant as well. She moved to England in the 1930s to attend the University of Oxford. This experience opened her mind to different political ideas and philosophies.

During her studies at Oxford, Indira became actively involved in the Indian Students' Union. She took part in various discussions and events that focused on India's political situation. Activism became a strong part of her identity as she connected with other students who shared her passion for social justice and freedom for India. This involvement laid the groundwork for her later political career.

In 1942, Indira married Feroze Gandhi, a Parsi journalist and activist, despite some opposition from her family. Feroze was supportive throughout Indira's career, but had his own political career. The couple had two sons. Rajiv Gandhi (1944–1991), who later became Prime Minister of India, and Sanjay Gandhi (1946–1980), who was a controversial political figure (The Editors of Encyclopedia Britannica, 2019).

In this year, 1942, Indira also returned from England to India. By this time, the country was in the midst of a significant struggle for independence. The impact of World War II had also affected India. Indira worked alongside her father and became active in the Indian National Congress. She played a role in organizing efforts to gain freedom from British rule. Her early experiences taught her the importance of commitment to a cause, a trait that she would carry throughout her life.

Indira Gandhi transformed modern India with her role in women's political representation. As the first and only female Prime Minister of India, her ascent to power in a predominantly male-dominated political landscape was nothing short of groundbreaking. Her leadership demonstrated that women could indeed occupy high political offices, serving as a beacon of possibility for aspiring female leaders across the globe. Breaking through the gender barriers of a patriarchal society, Gandhi navigated through the complexities of Indian politics with a tenacity that inspired countless women to envisage their potential within political spheres previously considered inaccessible.

Once in power, Indira Gandhi's leadership focused on progressive economic policies aimed at uplifting marginalized groups and promoting self-reliance among citizens. Recognizing the importance of women's empowerment as a valuable part of national development, she enacted several key policies intended to enhance the economic conditions of women and other disadvantaged communities. Through initiatives like the 20-Point Programme, Gandhi sought to tackle poverty and spur economic growth by addressing issues such as land redistribution, housing, and employment. These opportunities enhanced her commitment to social equality and her understanding of the critical role that women play in the nation's progress (MITRA, 2013).

Gandhi's efforts had an undeniable impact on the global stage, inspiring future generations of female leaders in developing countries. Her ability to hold one of the highest political positions in the world empowered and encouraged women worldwide, particularly in nations where female political participation was minimal or nonexistent. Gandhi's leadership style showcased the potential for women to govern effectively while facing immense political challenges. This legacy of empowerment continues to resonate today, influencing the pathways to leadership for women globally.

We can examine Gandhi's influence on international perspectives regarding women in leadership, identifying that her time in office coincided with significant geopolitical shifts. Her interactions with global leaders and her efforts on the international front inspire us by highlighting that contributions from women can make a real change in world affairs, setting an example for all of us to follow. Consequently, Gandhi's leadership left a lasting mark on the perceptions of women in politics, leading to gradual shifts in gender dynamics within government structures around the world. Indira Gandhi was assassinated in 1984, and her political role was taken over by her son, Rajiv. She was killed by her own bodyguards, Beant Singh and Satwant Singh, who were members of the Sikh community. The assassination was a direct retaliation for Operation Blue Star, a controversial military operation she had ordered earlier that year (The Editors of Encyclopedia Britannica, 2019).

# Angela Merkel's Leadership in Germany and Beyond

Angela Merkel (1954) is a notable leader recognized for being the first female Chancellor of Germany, serving for 16 years and playing a crucial role in shaping European and global politics through her pragmatic approach to issues such as the economy, immigration, and climate change.

Angela Merkel was born on July 8, 1954, in Hamburg, West Germany. She moved to East Germany with her family when she was just a few weeks old. Her father, a Lutheran minister, Horst Kasner, accepted a position in the East, which meant that Angela grew up in a very different environment than many of her West German peers. Her mother, Herlind Kasner, was a Latin and English teacher. Angela had two younger siblings: a brother, Marcus, and a sister, Irene. This early life in East Germany shaped her views and experiences. The isolation and different political climate of the East influenced her critical thinking and boosted her understanding of governance (Petrikowski, 2019).

Merkel excelled in school, showing particular talent in mathematics and the sciences. After graduating from high school, and went on to study physics at the University of Leipzig. This education was significant for both her knowledge and her analytical mindset. Studying in East Germany at a time when the country was heavily influenced by Soviet ideology meant that her education had a distinct political context.

Merkel was married twice. In 1977, at age 23, Angela married fellow physicist Ulrich Merkel. The couple divorced in 1982 but remained on amicable terms. In 1998, she married Joachim Sauer, a chemistry professor. Sauer is known for his low public profile, often referred to as the "Phantom of the Opera" due to his aversion to the spotlight. Merkel does not have children but is a stepmother to Sauer's two adult sons from a previous relationship (Petrikowski, 2019).

Merkel completed her doctorate in physics in 1986. Her thesis was about quantum chemistry, a topic that requires logical thinking and attention to detail. These skills would later serve her well in politics, as she made decisions based on solid evidence. After her studies, she worked for the Academy of Sciences in East Germany, where she specialized in research. Her work helped her gain insights into the scientific world, as well as the complexities of collaboration and innovation.

Soon after, the fall of the Berlin Wall in 1989 dramatically changed Merkel's life and career. Like many East Germans, she was swept up in the wave of change that came with reunification. She got involved in politics shortly after this event, joining the newly formed Democratic Awakening party. This move signified her desire to be part of the new political landscape. Her early involvement in politics introduced her to important figures and helped her establish a network.

In 1990, her party merged with the Christian Democratic Union (CDU), which was one of the major political parties in West Germany. This was a pivotal moment for Merkel. She quickly rose through the ranks of the CDU, demonstrating a knack for negotiation and governance. By 1991, she was appointed Minister for Women and Youth, and later she became Minister for the Environment. These roles helped her build a reputation as a capable leader who could handle complex issues.

As Minister for the Environment, Merkel created valuable policies related to environmental protection and energy. She helped shape Germany's approach to renewable energy, a topic that would persist throughout her career. This commitment to environmental issues would later be reflected in her policies as Chancellor, as she emphasized the importance of sustainable development.

Merkel's rise to power culminated in 2005 when she became the first female Chancellor of Germany. This moment was historic for her gender, and it also signals a symbolic shift that represented a transformation in the country. Her leadership style was often characterized by pragmatism and caution. Merkel focused on achieving consensus and was known for her careful decision-making process (Petrikowski, 2019).

Under her chancellorship, Germany faced numerous challenges, including the Eurozone crisis. Merkel's approach was to promote stability and responsibility. She advocated for measures that required countries to adhere to strict budgetary discipline. This was a contentious issue, but Merkel believed that strong financial governance was crucial for the health of the European economy. Her decisions often sparked debates, showcasing her ability to navigate complex political landscapes.

One of her notable policies was her response to the refugee crisis in 2015. As thousands of displaced people sought refuge in Europe, Merkel made the controversial decision to open Germany's borders. She believed that it was a moral obligation to help those in need. This decision drew both praise and criticism, shedding light on the balancing act she often performed between ethical considerations and practical governance.

Throughout her occupancy, Merkel was also active on the global stage. She attended numerous international summits and established herself as a key player in European and global politics. Her leadership prioritized international cooperation, especially in matters such as climate change. Merkel's commitment to multilateralism (when multiple countries are working together to achieve a common goal) helped reinforce Germany's position as a leader in European affairs. Through her advocacy, Merkel effectively demonstrated how women leaders can engage deeply with global matters, pushing beyond mere symbolic gestures to effect real change on an international scale (Marsh & Escritt, 2024).

Beyond her political achievements, Merkel has been known for her personal qualities. She is often described as pragmatic, resilient, and approachable. Her academic background and experience in science provided her with a unique perspective, allowing her to tackle issues with a level-headed approach. This reputation led many to view her as a stabilizing force in times of uncertainty.

Her journey from a young girl in East Germany to the highest office in the country is a testament to her determination and adaptability. Merkel's life proves to us that personal history, education, and societal changes can shape an influential leader. Each step of her path has contributed to her understanding of politics and governance, fostering a legacy that will be studied for years to come.

Angela Merkel's position as Germany's Chancellor stands as proof of the transformative power of leadership grounded in competence and practicality. Her journey from a scientist to one of the world's most influential political figures emphasizes the importance of analytical skills to challenge traditional gender biases in political realms. Merkel's rise showcases an era where expertise triumphed over preconceived notions of gender roles as she navigated the complexities of governance with precision and logic.

Merkel's methodical approach was particularly evident during the 2008 financial crisis. As countries around the globe experienced economic turmoil, Merkel emerged as a stabilizing force in Europe. Her policies helped Germany to weather the storm, and it also boosted confidence across the Eurozone. By skillfully balancing austerity measures and reliable support, Merkel challenged entrenched stereotypes that questioned women's capabilities in managing large-scale economic crises. This period revealed her ability to make tough decisions while maintaining the social fabric of the nation, strengthening her reputation as a leader who could navigate through turbulent waters with calm and resolve.

Another significant moment of Merkel's leadership was her commitment to democratic principles, even when confronting formidable geopolitical tensions. Her stance during the NATO summit in 2008, where she opposed offering Ukraine future membership, showcased her strategic vision. Though criticized by some, her decision was grounded in a long-term vision of maintaining regional stability. Merkel used this approach for her broader strategy: prioritizing calculated diplomacy over impulsive action, a quality that earned respect among global leaders and allowed her to maintain Germany's position as a critical player on the world stage (Marsh & Escritt, 2024).

Reflecting on Merkel's legacy teaches us how her leadership has paved the way for future generations of women in politics. As Germany's first female chancellor, Merkel became a symbol of what women can achieve in high office, thereby inspiring countless young girls and aspiring female leaders worldwide. Her occupation redefined expectations and provided guidance for women globally to lead nations successfully through multiple crises without compromising their inherent values or adopting traditionally masculine traits (Semenova, J., 2021).

Merkel's administration also boosted the representation of women within governmental roles. Her ability to mentor and promote female colleagues into significant positions of power showed her dedication to creating an environment where women could thrive and influence policy decisions meaningfully. While some critics argue that she could have done more to directly address gender inequalities domestically, the structural changes during her era created opportunities for many women to access leadership roles that were previously inaccessible.

Merkel stepped down from her position as Chancellor in 2021, ending a remarkable 16-year tenure. As Merkel's chancellorship concluded, her influence on both national and international stages continued to resonate. Her declaration of feminism, although later in her career, signified her acknowledgment of the ongoing struggle for gender equality and her solidarity with those striving for it. This act further cemented her as a figure of inspiration and a role model for women everywhere, demonstrating that leadership does not necessitate sacrificing your identity or beliefs (Marsh & Escritt, 2024).

# Julia Gillard's Tenure as Australia's Prime Minister

Julia Gillard (1961) is a trailblazing figure as the first female Prime Minister of Australia, known for her leadership in implementing significant educational reforms and advocating for gender equality while facing challenges related to her role as a woman in a historically male-dominated political landscape.

Julia Gillard was born on September 29, 1961, in Barry, Wales, United Kingdom. She was the second daughter of John Gillard, and Moira Gillard, a homemaker. She had one older sister, Alison. Her family emigrated to Australia in 1966 when Julia was five years old to escape economic hardship and seek a warmer climate for her health. As a child, Julia suffered from bronchopneumonia, which was also an influential factor in their relocation (Bhardwaj, G., 2019).

Her early life in Wales played a significant role in shaping her character and values. Julia grew up in a working-class family. Her father worked as a carpenter, and her mother was a teacher. This environment instilled in her the values of hard work and education from a very young age. Adjusting to a new country was not easy for her family.

They had to learn to navigate life in Australia while also maintaining their Welsh roots. Julia attended school in Australia and quickly learned to adapt to her new surroundings.

In school, Julia showed a keen interest in learning. She was an avid reader and excelled in subjects like English and history. Julia was not just focused on her studies; she was also involved in various activities. She participated in debating competitions, which helped her develop strong public speaking skills. These skills would later become essential in her political career.

As she grew older, Julia became increasingly aware of the social issues affecting her community. She volunteered in different social justice programs during high school. This involvement sparked her interest in politics. She began to understand the power of political action and how it could affect change.

After finishing high school, Julia attended the University of Melbourne. She studied arts and law, a combination that fueled her passion for social justice and public policy. At university, Julia was active in student politics. She joined the Australian Union of Students and became involved in many campaigns advocating for education reform and workers' rights. This experience gave her a deeper understanding of political processes and the importance of advocacy.

Julia graduated with her law degree in 1986. Not long after, she began her career as a lawyer. She worked as a solicitor and specialized in industrial relations. Her legal background provided her with a robust understanding of workplace issues, which would prove valuable in her later political roles. Julia's time as a lawyer allowed her to connect with various stakeholders and learn about the challenges facing different communities.

In 1998, Julia entered politics when she was elected as the Member for Lalor. This marked the beginning of her long and distinguished political career. She quickly made a name for herself within the Labor Party. Her work in the shadow cabinet focused on education and health issues close to her heart. Julia's early experiences laid the groundwork for her future leadership roles.

Her passion for education reform was evident in her policies. Julia believed that education was the key to breaking the cycle of poverty. She pushed for initiatives that would make education more accessible for all Australians. Her focus on improving educational outcomes started during her time as a Member of Parliament, and she continued to drive this agenda throughout her career.

Julia's leadership qualities emerged as she continued to gain experience. She became Deputy Prime Minister in 2007 under Prime Minister Kevin Rudd. This role allowed her to influence policies at the highest level. She learned the intricacies of running a government and managing a diverse team. Her experience during these formative years helped prepare her for her future as Prime Minister (Williams, B. 2020).

In 2010, Julia Gillard made history by becoming Australia's first female Prime Minister. This achievement was significant not only for her but for the entire nation. It demonstrated that women could hold the highest office in the country and be effective leaders. Julia's rise to power was a transformative moment in Australian politics and served as an inspiration for many (Williams, B. 2020).

Throughout her time as Prime Minister, Julia focused on several key issues. She sought to improve access to education and healthcare, believing that these were fundamental rights for all citizens. Her policies aimed to create a more inclusive society where everyone had the opportunity to succeed. Julia faced numerous challenges during her tenure, but her determination never wavered.

Julia's childhood experiences and upbringing played an essential role in her political philosophy. Growing up in a working-class family taught her the importance of empathy and understanding. She always kept these values close to her heart as she navigated the political landscape. Julia knew that her background resonated with many Australians, which motivated her to serve the public.

Her journey from a small town in Wales to the highest political office in Australia illustrates the power of perseverance and hard work. It serves as a reminder that anyone can achieve their dreams, regardless of their background. Julia Gillard's story is one of dedication, leadership, and trailblazing for the future generations of female leaders in politics.

Julia's achievements did not go unnoticed. After leaving the office, she continued to advocate for education and gender equality. She worked with numerous organizations and spoke at events around the world. Her experiences and insights have positioned her as a respected figure in global discussions on women's rights and leadership.

Many may wonder how Julia maintained her resilience amidst the challenges she faced. It was, in part, her strong sense of purpose and commitment to her ideals. Julia Gillard's path is a testament to the impact of a supportive home environment and the importance of education in shaping a person's future. Her life serves as a powerful example of the choices one can make to affect change within society.

Through her dedication to public service, Julia Gillard has inspired many to pursue their passions and strive for a better world. Her journey reflects the importance of understanding one's roots while aspiring for greatness. Julia continues to be a source of inspiration for many aspiring leaders and advocates. Her story emphasizes that with hard work and determination, anything is possible.

Julia Gillard's journey as Australia's first female Prime Minister was not only a personal triumph but a landmark moment in the nation's history, symbolizing the breaking of long-standing barriers in a predominantly male political landscape. Her ascent to leadership sent a potent message to women and girls across Australia and beyond, inspiring them to envision their potential roles in governance and other arenas traditionally dominated by men. This transformative achievement paved the way for more inclusive aspirations toward leadership, fostering a renewed sense of possibility among upcoming generations of women leaders.

During her tenure from 2010 to 2013, Gillard championed significant legislative actions that fortified educational access and women's rights, key issues she prioritized throughout her career. One of her notable achievements was the introduction of the Gonski school funding reforms, which aimed at ensuring all children had equitable access to quality education, regardless of their socio-economic background. This approach underscored her belief in education as a powerful equalizer and a critical tool for empowering future generations. By reinforcing educational opportunities, she laid the groundwork for a more inclusive society where meritocracy trumps gender bias, setting a benchmark for future policy-making.

Gillard's advocacy extended into the realm of workplace gender equality, an area she vigorously pursued through various reforms. These included initiatives aiming to close the gender pay gap, improve workplace conditions for women, and address systemic discrimination across industries. Her push for legislative changes resonated with many women, igniting broader discussions on how gender equality could be integrated into the core of workplace policies and cultures across the globe. This reshaping of conversations marked a shift toward recognizing the importance of equal representation and treatment in professional spaces.

One of the most defining moments of Gillard's prime ministership came with her iconic "Misogyny Speech" delivered on October 9, 2012. Addressing Tony Abbott's hypocrisy and sexism in Parliament, Gillard's speech became a global sensation, shedding light on the entrenched sexism women often face in politics. Initially critiqued by some within the Australian media, the speech struck a chord internationally, amplifying conversations about gender bias and the struggles female leaders endure (Williams, 2020). It was a brave revelation of the challenges within the corridors of power and inspired many to question and challenge the status quo regarding women's treatment in leadership roles. This moment not only solidified her legacy in Australian political history, but also became a touchstone for discussing sexism and patriarchy worldwide.

Beyond her political career, Gillard continued her unwavering commitment to advocating for girls' education and women's rights. After leaving office, she took on global roles that allowed her to influence educational policies and promote mental health awareness. She chaired the Global Partnership for Education, an organization dedicated to increasing educational opportunities for children in developing countries, particularly emphasizing the education of girls. Such endeavors highlight her enduring dedication to driving progressive policies that aim to create more equitable societies.

Her work post-premiership further showcases her ability to translate past experiences and insights into actionable change on an international scale. By leveraging her platform, Gillard has continuously emphasized the necessity of education as an integral element for achieving gender equality worldwide. Her efforts serve as a reminder of the importance of sustaining advocacy beyond political office and influencing policies that benefit women and girls globally (Bhardwaj, 2019). Through these initiatives, she not only maintains her relevance as a significant figure in contemporary discourse on gender equality, but also continues to inspire a new generation of activists and leaders committed to progressive change.

Julia Gillard has never married and does not have children, a decision she has spoken about publicly, acknowledging the sacrifices involved in her political life. She continues to actively pursue her advocacy works and efforts, especially in education and health.

# Tsai Ing-Wen's Impact as Taiwan's President

Tsai Ing-Wen (1956) is a remarkable leader as the first female President of Taiwan, known for her strong stance on Taiwan's sovereignty and democracy while promoting progressive reforms in areas such as social policy and women's rights, significantly shaping the island's identity and international relations.

Tsai Ing-wen was born on August 31, 1956, in Taipei City, Taiwan. She grew up in a modest family that valued education and hard work. Tsai was the youngest of eight siblings, which meant that she had the opportunity to learn from her older brothers and sisters. Her father, Tsai Chieh-Sheng, was a successful businessman, and her mother, Chang Chin-Fong, was his fourth wife (Pletcher, 2019). From an early age, Tsai showed a keen interest in learning. Her parents encouraged her curiosity by providing her with books and educational materials.

This nurturing environment helped Tsai develop a strong foundation for her academic future.

Unfortunately, during her childhood, Tsai faced various challenges. Taiwan was under martial law, which meant that political freedoms were limited. Many families were affected by the political climate, and Tsai's family was no different. Despite these challenges, her parents reinforced the importance of perseverance and determination. They taught her to focus on her studies and to work hard for her goals and values that would later influence her political career.

As Tsai Ing-wen grew older, she excelled in school. Her hard work paid off when she earned a scholarship to study at National Taiwan University. This was a significant achievement for her and her family. At university, she pursued a degree in law, which laid the groundwork for her future career. Tsai's education allowed her to gain a deeper understanding of the legal system, society, and politics. This knowledge would later play a crucial role in her life as she entered public service (Pletcher, 2019).

After finishing her degree in Taiwan, Tsai continued her education abroad. She attended Cornell University in the United States, where she earned a master's degree in 1980. She then studied law at the London School of Economics and was awarded a Ph.D. in law from the University of London in 1984 (*LSE Statement on PhD of Dr Tsai Ing-Wen*, 2019). This experience exposed her to different political ideas and systems. Tsai was able to see the world from a new perspective, deepening her understanding of democracy and governance. These experiences shaped her beliefs and values, urging her to pursue a path in politics. Tsai Ing-wen has never been married and does not have children. She has described herself as a work-focused individual, dedicating her life to public service.

Tsai returned to Taiwan after completing her studies and began working in various roles within the government. One of her first significant positions was in the Mainland Affairs Council, where she worked on cross-strait relations. This experience helped her understand the complexities of Taiwan's relationship with China. Tsai became passionate about promoting Taiwan's interests and ensuring its voice was heard on the international stage (Pletcher, 2019).

Over the years, Tsai continued to climb the political ladder. She served in several key positions, including as the chairperson of the Mainland Affairs Council and the Vice Premier. Each role was built upon her previous experiences, allowing her to gain vital insights into Taiwan's political landscape. Her work focused on fostering dialogue and understanding between different political entities while advocating for Taiwan's unique identity.

In the political landscape of Taiwan, Tsai Ing-wen's historic election as the first female president in 2016 was a monumental achievement that challenged entrenched gender roles and initiated significant change. This milestone transcended symbolism; it marked a shift toward greater gender equality and demonstrated to Taiwanese society—and the world—that women could effectively lead a nation. Tsai's triumph over traditional societal expectations underscored her role as a trailblazer for women's representation in Asia, setting a precedent that encouraged more women to pursue leadership positions.

Tsai's presidency not only shattered gender norms but also revolutionized domestic policies to focus on issues previously sidelined in national discussions. Her dedication to championing women's rights is evident in her initiatives aimed at improving work-life balance and providing support for working mothers. By pushing these critical issues to the forefront of national dialogue, Tsai has created an environment where women's voices are increasingly heard and valued. Under her leadership, Taiwan saw reforms that reflected her commitment to gender equality, reinforcing the importance of integrating women's perspectives into policy-making processes.

Understanding the intricacies of balancing a career with family responsibilities, Tsai advocated for policies that allowed women to thrive both personally and professionally. Her administration introduced programs to enhance maternity leave benefits and childcare services, making it feasible for more women to participate fully in the workforce without sacrificing family obligations. Such measures have had a palpable impact on society, demonstrating that government support can empower women to achieve their potential and contribute to national progress.

In addition to her transformative domestic policies, Tsai has adeptly navigated the international stage by emphasizing Taiwan's sovereignty and promoting global gender equality. Amidst geopolitical tensions, particularly with China, her foreign policy approach has been one of resilience and assertiveness. Tsai harnessed soft power strategies to advocate for Taiwan's identity and independence, positioning the country as a beacon for democratic values in Asia. She artfully balanced diplomacy and advocacy, ensuring that Taiwan's interests were protected while forging alliances that highlighted the importance of equality across borders.

One notable example of her diplomatic prowess was Taiwan's response during the COVID-19 pandemic, where Tsai's leadership was crucial in managing the crisis efficiently. Her administration offered assistance to countries in need, showcasing Taiwan as a model of cooperation and capability—an impressive feat despite the island's exclusion from the World Health Organization. In this context, Tsai's presidency became synonymous with effective governance, earning her recognition and respect globally and within Taiwan.

Moreover, Tsai's endeavor to promote gender equality wasn't confined to national boundaries; she extended her vision internationally. Her tenure has seen increased collaboration in endeavors that address gender disparities worldwide, signaling Taiwan's willingness to engage in global dialogues on equality. By doing so, Tsai has positioned herself and her country as advocates for change, further inspiring future leaders to adopt similar stances.

The legacy of Tsai Ing-wen's presidency extends beyond immediate policy changes; it has fundamentally shifted perceptions of women in leadership roles throughout Asia. Her success has paved the way for aspiring female political candidates, emboldening them to challenge the status quo and redefine the landscape of political leadership. The visibility and effectiveness of her administration serve as powerful evidence that women can lead with competence and grace in traditionally male-dominated spheres.

As Tsai continues to guide Taiwan through complex challenges, her influence remains a testament to the strength of progressive leadership. Her ability to tackle pressing national issues while advocating for gender equality exemplifies the multifaceted demands of contemporary governance. Tsai Ing-wen's presidency stands as a significant chapter not only in Taiwan's history but also in the broader narrative of women's global leadership.

Tsai's impact reaches far beyond political achievements; she represents a shift in cultural attitudes toward gender roles and leadership capabilities. Through her efforts, she has opened doors for future generations, encouraging young girls and women to aspire to influential positions and to perceive themselves as capable changemakers. Embodying resilience and innovation in her leadership has given Tsai Ing-wen the platform to create a legacy that will continue to inspire and motivate women globally. Her calm and steady leadership style, coupled with her academic and professional achievements, makes her a role model for women in politics worldwide (Pletcher, 2019).

# Concluding Thoughts

This chapter ventures through the remarkable journeys of women who have navigated their way to leadership roles in global politics, each leaving a lasting impact on their societies and beyond. The stories of Indira Gandhi, Angela Merkel, Julia Gillard, and Tsai Ing-Wen inspire us with the transformative power of female leadership in traditionally male-dominated spaces. Breaking down these barriers and reshaping the political landscapes of their respective nations, these women have influenced domestic policies and set new standards for international diplomacy and governance. Their leadership styles, rooted in resilience, pragmatism, and advocacy for equality, teach us that we can successfully drive change while confronting unique challenges.

Through their efforts, despite facing adversity, these leaders have inspired future generations and shifted perceptions of women's capabilities in governance. This chapter covered some ways these remarkable figures have encouraged young women to pursue influential roles across the globe. By examining their tenures, we gain valuable insights into how these women have achieved progress toward gender equality and social justice, providing role models for those aspiring to create a more equitable world. As we reflect on their contributions, it becomes evident that the impact of their leadership inspires and empowers communities globally.

# Chapter 5:
# Cultural Icons and Feminist Artistry

Exploring cultural icons and feminist artistry illuminates the voices that have shaped modern art and society. This chapter discusses how notable women artists have used their creative platforms to reflect on gender, identity, and social justice, shedding light on the broader cultural discourse. Through their unique perspectives, these artists challenge traditional norms and inspire change, creating a narrative that transcends time and culture. Each artist featured in this exploration brings a distinct approach to addressing feminist themes, showcasing the power of art as both a mirror and a catalyst for societal transformation. Through this chapter, we will embark on a journey through the lives and works of influential figures, such as Frida Kahlo, Merata Mita, and Yayoi Kusama.

# Frida Kahlo's Art and Its Reflection on Gender and Identity

Frida Kahlo (1907-1954) was an amazing artist celebrated for her deeply personal and symbolic paintings that explore themes of identity, pain, and feminism, making her an enduring icon of individuality and resilience in the art world.

Frida Kahlo was born on July 6, 1907, in Coyoacán, a suburb of Mexico City. Her birth took place during a time when Mexico was undergoing significant social and political changes. This period would influence her life and her artwork. Frida was the daughter of a German father, Guillermo Kahlo, and a Mexican mother, Matilde Calderón. This multicultural heritage shaped her identity, as she often explored themes of identity, culture, and belonging in her work, reflecting the complexities of her own background (*Frida Kahlo Biography*, 2002).

Growing up, Frida experienced both joy and hardship. She had three sisters, and while they were close, Frida often felt different. Her family was not particularly wealthy, but they were comfortable enough. Frida was introduced to art at an early age by her father, who was a photographer. He encouraged her to explore her creative side, and this laid the groundwork for her future artistic endeavors. However, Frida's childhood was not without challenges. At the age of six, she contracted polio, which left her with a lifelong disability in her right leg. This experience of illness made her more aware of her body and its limitations, a theme that reappeared throughout her life and art.

During her adolescence, Frida attended the prestigious National Preparatory School. This environment allowed her to pursue her education and make lasting friendships. There, she became active in politics and developed a passion for socialism. She was exposed to new ideas and cultures, which influenced her later work. One of her close friends was the famous Mexican muralist Diego Rivera. Their friendship would later blossom into a tumultuous relationship that would beautifully impact her life and art.

Frida's political engagement shaped her views and artistic expression. She admired the efforts of the Mexican Revolution and the fight for social justice. These ideals often found their way into her artwork, where she addressed themes like inequality and identity. Frida's paintings are known for their vibrant colors and emotional depth, often portraying her pain, emotions, and experiences. This was particularly evident after the tragic bus accident in 1925, which changed her life forever.

The bus accident left her with severe injuries, including a broken spine and pelvis. Frida spent months in recovery, during which she began to paint more seriously. It was during this time that she established her unique style, which combined elements of surrealism, folk art, and Mexican culture. Through her paintings, she confronted her suffering and the societal expectations imposed on women. For example, in one of her famous works, "The Two Fridas," she portrayed her dual identity—one representing her European heritage and the other her Mexican roots.

Frida's complex relationship with her identity continued as she navigated through her life. After recovering from her injuries, she married Diego Rivera in 1931. Their marriage was filled with lots of love and turmoil. Frida admired Rivera's work, but she also faced her own challenges in the shadow of his fame. This struggle led her to explore her own creative voice, resulting in powerful self-portraits conveying her emotions and experiences (*Frida Kahlo and the Legacy of Feminist Ideology,* 2022).

Throughout the years, Frida's health continued to decline. She endured numerous surgeries and faced constant pain, yet her passion for art never waned. She utilized art as a means of coping with her struggles, enabling her to express her innermost feelings. In her works, she often included symbols of pain and suffering, such as a broken heart or her own image distorted in reflections.

Kahlo's work meant more than mere representation; it became a medium through which she articulated her experiences as a woman, a disability, and a Mexican artist. The imagery in her paintings often referenced her indigenous heritage, emphasizing her roots and cultural significance. Frida believed in the importance of preserving her culture, which was integral to her identity.

In addition to her personal struggles, Frida was a strong advocate for women's rights and the representation of women in art. She defied societal norms and expectations, challenging the traditional roles of women in her time. Frida's art often depicted the female experience with raw honesty, illustrating the complexities of womanhood, love, and suffering.

Her legacy today can be seen far beyond her paintings, as she has become a symbol of feminism and resilience. Frida Kahlo's journey reflects the struggles and triumphs of a woman who dared to live authentically in a world that often tried to confine her. Her life story continues to inspire countless individuals to embrace their truths and express their identities without fear.

Kahlo passed away on July 13, 1954, leaving behind a rich artistic legacy that captivates audiences worldwide. Her life's journey—from her humble beginnings to her status as a cultural icon—resonates with many. Frida's upbringing and background played a fundamental role in shaping the artist she became. Her experiences of pain, love, identity, and culture remain central themes in her work, inviting viewers to reflect on the complexities of their own lives and identities (Frida Kahlo, 2024).

## Merata Mita's Films on Māori Culture and Social Justice

Merata Mita (1942-2010) was a remarkable filmmaker and activist known for being the first Maori woman to direct a feature film, using her platform to tell indigenous stories and advocate for Maori rights, significantly impacting New Zealand's cultural landscape and women's representation in film.

Merata Mita was born into a family as the third of nine children and had a traditional rural Māori upbringing that deeply shaped her identity and her future work as a filmmaker. Growing up in New Zealand, she was surrounded by a rich cultural environment that influenced her perspective on storytelling. Mita was of Māori descent, which played a significant role in her life. The Māori culture is known for its strong emphasis on community, tradition, and connection to the land. This cultural backdrop would later inform her creative pursuits and her commitment to representing Māori stories authentically (Zimmer, n.d.).

Her childhood experiences often inspired her work. During her formative years, Mita faced many challenges, including navigating a society that did not always embrace her cultural identity. These experiences motivated her to explore themes of identity and belonging in her films. Understanding the struggles of her community, she became passionate about shedding light on the issues faced by Māori people. Her early life fueled a desire to craft stories that reflected her experiences and perspectives.

Family significantly influenced Mita's upbringing. Her parents instilled in her the importance of storytelling, a tradition that is central to many Māori families. They likely shared tales from their ancestry, emphasizing the significance of passing down knowledge through generations. These stories contributed to Mita's understanding of her cultural heritage and influenced her decision to pursue a career in film. She recognized the power of storytelling as a means of educating others and preserving her culture.

Mita's adolescent years were filled with exploration and discovery. She became increasingly aware of the limitations placed on her and her peers within societal structures. This awareness ignited her passion for activism, as she sought to challenge stereotypes and fight for the rights of her community. During this time, she began to appreciate the impact of film as a medium for change. It was not just about entertainment for her; it was a way to express ideas, challenge perceptions, and inspire others.

Her first encounters with the film were powerful. Exposure to cinema opened her eyes to new storytelling possibilities. Mita experienced a mix of emotions when she watched films that portrayed Māori life. While some films celebrated aspects of her culture, others perpetuated harmful stereotypes. This division fueled her desire to create her own narratives that would represent her community with authenticity and respect. She felt a responsibility to create films that would entertain and educate audiences about Māori culture.

As she continued her journey, Mita started to connect with fellow aspiring filmmakers. This connection led to the formation of a network focused on supporting Indigenous storytellers. Collaborating with others who shared her vision allowed her to hone her craft and explore different perspectives. These relationships made a huge impact on her growth as a filmmaker, and they provided her with opportunities to learn. Mita's commitment to collaboration encouraged many emerging female filmmakers to share their own stories and talent.

In her personal life, Mita also balanced the responsibilities of her family. Becoming a mother while navigating her career presented its own set of challenges. However, she remained determined to pursue her passion for filmmaking. Mita demonstrated that it is possible to grow professionally while nurturing personal relationships. Her experiences raised awareness about the experiences and sacrifices of women in creative fields, especially those from marginalized backgrounds.

Merata Mita is a remarkable figure in the history of filmmaking, breaking new ground as one of the first Māori women directors and using her lens to amplify Indigenous voices. Mita's documentaries are powerful educational tools that tackle issues valuable to the Māori community with a raw, unfiltered approach. Films such as "Patu!"—which documented the protests against the 1981 Springbok Tour in New Zealand—are a great example of her work committed to addressing social justice (Tappenden & Shelton, n.d.). These works display the struggles faced by Māori people, providing them with a voice that draws awareness. This reframing breaks down stereotypes and promotes a deeper understanding of indigenous experiences, creating empathy and awareness among audiences far beyond New Zealand's shores.

Her body of work brings light to the resilience and strength of Māori women, portraying characters that embody the spirit of advocacy and empowerment. Through her films, Mita challenges traditional gender roles and emphasizes the importance of community support in the fight for Indigenous women's rights. Displaying these themes through films has inspired marginalized groups worldwide, helping other Indigenous populations' voices speak their truths.

Merata Mita's legacy has also had indirect contributions to feminism, by advocating for diversity and representation in media. Mita's advocacy for the decolonization and indigenization of cinema has helped her redefine how stories should be told (Schallenkammer, 2024). She viewed filmmaking as a form of modern storytelling close to the role of the kaikōrero on the marae ātea, reclaiming narrative authority from non-indigenous viewpoints. This enriched cultural context and authenticity makes Mita's work resonate deeply with those seeking to understand and appreciate Indigenous histories and identities.

Her ability to navigate and challenge the male-dominated film industry added another layer to her activism. Despite facing significant opposition, as seen through her candid discussions about the industry's dynamics, Mita never compromised her vision or values (Tappenden & Shelton, n.d.). Her outspoken nature and determination to challenge entrenched systems paved the way for more equitable representation within the arts, setting a precedent for other Māori women and artists striving to tell their own stories authentically. Merata Mita passed away on May 31, 2010, at the age of 66. She died from complications related to her long battle with cancer, which she bravely faced while continuing to advocate for indigenous rights and cultural representation in media. The legacy she made for herself shows us how important it is to have diverse narratives that shape cultural discourse and promote inclusivity within the arts and in every other field.

# Yayoi Kusama's Influence on Modern Art

Yayoi Kusama (1929) is a renowned artist whose work has left a significant mark on the art world. She was born on March 22, 1929, in Matsumoto, Japan. Kusama grew up in a time and place where traditional values and expectations were strong. Her childhood was not easy, and she faced various challenges that shaped her into the artist she is today. Growing up in a conservative family, she experienced difficulties with her mental health, which made her into the artist she is today.

Kusama's childhood was filled with extreme experiences that influenced her art. As a child, she was forced by her mom to spy on her father's lovers, causing her trauma she still struggles with today. She used this anxiety and fear from these experiences to live through art (Tess in the City, 2020). She was particularly inspired by nature. As a child, she spent time in the countryside, surrounded by fields of flowers. These experiences left a lasting impression on her. She frequently recalled the vibrant colors of nature, which later appeared in her work. She also experienced hallucinations, which contributed to her unique perspective. These visions often included repetitive patterns, dots, and other forms that recur in her artwork.

At a young age, Kusama discovered her love for drawing. She started to sketch and paint, often using simple materials she found around her. This early exploration played a vital role in her artistic development. She attended the Kyoto School of Arts and Crafts, where she studied traditional Japanese painting. However, her desire to break free from traditional norms led her to experiment with different styles and techniques. She began blending Eastern and Western art influences, which became a hallmark of her later work.

In 1957, at the age of 28, Kusama moved to the United States to pursue her art career. New York City was a successful center for artists at that time, and she hoped to find her place within its vibrant scene (Woodham, 2017). The move was a significant shift for her. She encountered new ideas, people, and art movements that further shaped her vision. Living in America allowed her to explore her themes of infinity and obsession on a much larger scale. She became part of the avant-garde community, connecting with other influential artists such as Andy Warhol and Claes Oldenburg.

The transition to a new country was not easy for Kusama. She faced cultural differences and social challenges. Despite these hardships, she persevered. She found solace in creating art. Her work began to reflect her experiences, combining her psychological struggles with her artistic expression. The isolation she felt in America fueled her creativity. She created immersive installations using dots and mirrors, that invited viewers to experience her visions of infinity firsthand.

Kusama's artistic style evolved significantly over the years. She moved from the traditional Japanese painting techniques she learned in school to innovative modern art forms. Kusama's utilization of bold patterns, particularly polka dots, serves as more than just a signature motif; it is a visual representation of her internal struggles and triumphs. She often refers to her work as a way to find relief from her mental health challenges, transforming her pain into beautiful art. The repetitive nature of her work, such as in her Infinity Net series or her expansive Obliteration Rooms, symbolizes her battle with anxiety and hallucinations, offering a glimpse into the emotional landscapes she navigates (Subversive Sweetheart, 2017). This art style encourages viewers to reconsider preconceived notions about mental illness, often perceived negatively, and instead celebrate the creativity and passion it can inspire (Yayoi Kusama, 2024).

As the years went by, Kusama gained recognition for her unique style and perspective. Her art has been exhibited in numerous galleries and museums worldwide. Audiences have been captivated by the way she combines personal experiences with universal themes. She has become an influential figure in contemporary art, inspiring countless artists with her dedication and originality.

When taking a look into the influence of Yayoi Kusama on contemporary feminism, we should first consider her unique artistic style and its engagement with themes of infinity. Kusama's bold patterns and immersive installations are aesthetic choices that have deeply rooted expressions, exploring complex issues of mental health and identity. These elements portray women's unique experiences, making her work both a personal exploration and a broader commentary that resonates with many.

The concept of infinity in Kusama's work forms another valuable layer of her artistic story. When Kusama embeds this theme across her pieces, she symbolically unlocks countless possibilities for women. Her Infinity Mirror Rooms, where reflections seem endless, invite audiences to engage in introspection on empowerment and personal growth, inspiring women to see beyond immediate societal confines and toward infinite potential. These installations provide an immersive experience, surrounding viewers and blurring the lines between reality and perception, thus offering a powerful metaphor for boundless female achievement and self-exploration (Yayoi Kusama, 2024).

Kusama's art confronts societal stigma head-on, using her platform to dissolve traditional barriers in both art and society. During a time when the male-dominated art world often sidelined women and their voices, Kusama challenged these norms through her unapologetic expression of sexuality and gender themes. Her artwork boldly addresses traditional gender roles and the phallocentric power structures within society, as exemplified by her controversial happenings in New York City during the 1960s. These public performances, which utilized nudity and other provocative elements, subverted the oppressive male gaze and offered a feminist perspective of the status quo, setting a precedent for future activist art (Subversive Sweetheart, 2017).

Kusama's role as a cultural icon has paved pathways for future female artists. Her recognition and success in the global art sphere have elevated the discourse around women in art, proving that a woman's voice can resonate powerfully within this space. Her journey from a young artist in Japan to an internationally celebrated figure demonstrates the possibility of overcoming restrictive cultural expectations and influencing change on a global scale. This opens doors for emerging female artists who look to Kusama as a trailblazer and an example of how to merge personal storytelling with larger feminist dialogues (Yayoi Kusama, 2024).

Kusama's artistic practice has significantly contributed to redefining feminist art. She challenges conventional representations of femininity and offers a space for women and men to discuss women's rights and social justice. Through her works, she presents a connected perspective that bridges cultural divides between Japan and the Western world, showcasing how art can be a conduit for cross-cultural understanding and feminist advocacy. Her art speaks to diverse audiences, encouraging conversations that go beyond geographical boundaries and touch upon universal themes of equality and empowerment (Yayoi Kusama, 2024).

# Summary and Reflections

In this chapter, we've discussed the powerful ways women artists use their creativity to express feminist ideas and contribute uniquely to cultural discussions. Frida Kahlo's art transcends mere visual appeal by challenging traditional norms through deeply personal expressions of identity and feminine experience. Her incorporation of cultural motifs honors her Mexican heritage and also highlights the connection between feminism and cultural pride. Similarly, Merata Mita's groundbreaking films have amplified Indigenous voices and brought attention to Māori issues, intertwining social justice advocacy with authentic storytelling. Through their work, both Kahlo and Mita encourage reflection on our narratives and inspire a continued dialogue around women's rights and equality.

Yayoi Kusama's influence on contemporary art further illustrates how women artists challenge societal barriers and succeed in achieving female empowerment. Her bold patterns and exploration of infinite themes provide commentary that resonates with many women's experiences. Kusama's unapologetic approach to addressing gender and mental health issues dismantles traditional boundaries, offering a space for future generations to engage in valuable conversations about feminism. Together, the works of Kahlo, Mita, and Kusama act as beacons for all women seeking social justice. These artists demonstrate the long-lasting capacity of art to inspire change, bridge cultural divides, and promote gender equality worldwide.

# Chapter 6:
# Trailblazers of Social Justice

Trailblazers of social justice have significantly shaped the journey toward equal rights across various sectors over the decades. Their stories serve as a source of inspiration for many. These formidable women challenged societal and institutional norms, impacting change through their courage and determination. Their efforts have redirected conversations around social justice, education, environmentalism, and gender equality. They embody the spirit of activism that transcends boundaries and breaks down barriers, pushing societies toward greater inclusivity. By recognizing these significant causes, we can learn about the power of advocacy to transform individual struggles into movements that resonate on a global scale. Through their actions, these leaders have demonstrated how passion combined with perseverance can forge paths previously deemed impassable, setting precedents for future generations to embrace and build upon. Throughout this chapter, we will walk through the lives and legacies of key figures like Malala Yousafzai, Vigdís Finnbogadóttir, and Hanan Ashrawi.

# Malala Yousafzai's Fight for Education

Malala Yousafzai (1997) is an outstanding figure known for her courageous advocacy for girls' education, particularly in Pakistan, where she survived an assassination attempt by the Taliban, ultimately becoming a global symbol of resilience and the fight for equality in education.

Malala Yousafzai was born on July 12, 1997, in Mingora, a city in the Swat Valley of Pakistan. She has two younger brothers, Khushal Yousafzai and Atal Yousafzai. This area is known for its stunning landscapes, including mountains and rivers, but it also faced significant challenges, particularly around the time of Malala's childhood. Growing up in such a picturesque yet chaotic setting shaped much of her early life and character. The region was influenced by various factors, including religion, culture, and politics, which also contributed to Malala's upbringing.

From a young age, Malala was deeply influenced by her family's values. Her father, Ziauddin Yousafzai, was an educator and a social activist. He ran a school, which inspired Malala's love for learning. He believed that education is a vital tool for empowerment, and he instilled this belief in his daughter. Malala often accompanied her father to the school, where she witnessed the transformative power of education firsthand. This experience ignited her passion for knowledge and her understanding of its importance, especially for girls in her community. Malala's mother, Tor Pakai, also played an essential role in her life, although she did not have the same educational opportunities as her husband. Despite this, she emphasized the importance of education and supported her daughter's ambitions.

As she grew older, the political climate in Pakistan became increasingly unstable. The rise of the Taliban in the Swat Valley brought severe restrictions on education, particularly for girls. Schools were attacked, and many were forced to close. Despite these threats, Malala bravely continued to advocate for education. At just eleven years old, she began writing a blog under a pseudonym for the BBC Urdu, sharing her experiences of life under Taliban rule. In her writings, she described the fear that pervaded her community and the impact of school closures on girls. This act of courage was both a personal expression and a rallying cry for girls everywhere who were denied education.

Malala Yousafzai's journey is a powerful voice in challenging entrenched societal norms. A quote from her famous speech at The United Nations Youth Assembly *"One child, one teacher, one book and one pen can change the world"*, has inspired many girls around the world (*Malala Addresses Youth Delegates in UN*, n.d.). This speech is filled with many inspiring words that we can hold on to in our journey toward change. Growing up in Pakistan's Khyber Pakhtunkhwa province, Malala recognized from a young age the significance of education, not just for personal growth but as a beacon of hope against patriarchal constraints. Her advocacy began amidst the harsh realities imposed by the Taliban, who sought to sever girls' access to education. Despite the dangers, she bravely spoke out through anonymous blog posts and public engagements, courageously amplifying the urgent need for educational rights in her community (Yousafzai 2024). This early defiance underscored the ability of one determined individual to potentially alter perceptions and initiate change within a society resistant to evolution.

In October 2012, Malal's activism took a devastating turn as she experienced a horrifying assassination attempt. At just 15 years old, this attack singled her out for opposing Taliban restrictions on female education, but instead of silencing her, it caused global attention. After surviving the gunshot wound and months of recovery, Malala transformed her traumatic experience into a driving force for global advocacy via the establishment of the Malala Fund. Through this organization, she symbolized resilience and unwavering dedication, turning personal adversity into a platform for widespread influence. The Malala Fund's mission—to ensure that every girl has access to 12 years of free, safe, and quality education—became a rallying cry that won international support and funding to enhance educational opportunities for girls worldwide through encouraging words from her same speech *"We call upon our sisters around the world—to be brave—to embrace the strength within themselves and realize their full potential"* (*Malala Yousafzai*, 2017).

In recognition of her outstanding courage and contributions to education advocacy, Malala was awarded the Nobel Peace Prize in December 2014 at the age of 17, making her the youngest-ever recipient of the prestigious honor. This accolade recognized her past endeavors and also placed her story at the forefront of global discussions about educational policy and youth involvement. Malala's recognition served as a powerful reminder of the importance of elevating youth voices in dialogues that shape educational frameworks and strategies. Her example articulated how young leaders can influence systemic changes and inspire generations to push for fair and equal access to education as a fundamental human right.

Malala's journey further emphasizes the connection between gender and education, displaying how they can be directly linked in the fight against injustice. Her advocacy covered education but also challenged structural inequalities and ingrained societal dynamics that reinforced gender imbalances. As she uses her platform to this day, Malala encourages others to confront and oppose injustices in their communities, thus transforming communities with her individual devotion to female equality. Her story inspires activists globally to identify and dismantle barriers that hinder girls' educational opportunities.

Lessons learned from Malala's journey emphasize the necessity of resilience and persistence in advocacy efforts. Her experience teaches an invaluable lesson: even when faced with overwhelming adversity, commitment to your cause can yield substantial impact. It offers powerful guidelines for activists aiming to create meaningful social change—showcasing the need for endurance when fighting for change. Her story also shows us how important it is to strategically use your platform to amplify your voice as a marginalized individual.

Malala's work also sheds light on the potent influence of storytelling in catalyzing activism. When we hear about her inspiring narrative, she personifies the struggles and aspirations of all of us who have experienced discrimination and have been denied basic rights. Her approach to inequality demonstrates how personal stories can compel empathy, drive engagement, and inspire action across diverse social contexts.

As Malala continues her efforts post-Oxford graduation, the global landscape of girls' education remains fraught with challenges. Her unwavering dedication and exemplary leadership continue to inspire hope and action. She calls upon people worldwide to join her fight for education and equality, emphasizing the communal responsibility to break down barriers and cultivate environments where all girls can learn and lead (Yousafzai, 2024). In doing so, Malala invites us to envision a world where education is universally accessible, breaking cycles of poverty and empowering future generations to transcend existing limitations.

# Vigdís Finnbogadóttir: The World's First Female Elected President

Vigdís Finnbogadóttir (1930) was the first female president of Iceland and the first woman to be democratically elected president in the world (Pruitt, 2020). She was born in 1930 in Reykjavík, Iceland. Vigdís was born into a well-educated home. She grew up during a time when Iceland was still establishing its identity as a nation after gaining independence from Denmark in 1944. This context of nation-building and cultural development surrounded her as she was growing up, sparking her interest in Icelandic culture, history, and politics (Brellan, 2019).

Vigdís was the daughter of a nurse who was a pioneering leader of the nursing profession in Iceland, and her father was a civil engineer (*Vigdís Finnbogadóttir*, 2020). This environment instilled in her the importance of education. Her mother's influence encouraged Vigdís to pursue her studies diligently (Brellan, 2019). Through her passion for the creative world, she served as director of the Reykjavík Theatre

Company (Leikfélag Reykjavíkur) between 1972 and 1980 (*Vigdís Finnbogadóttir*, 2020).

After graduating from Reykjavík College in 1949, she attended the University of Grenoble and the Sorbonne in France and the University of Uppsala in Sweden. At that time it was uncommon for girls in Iceland to study abroad. She also studied in Denmark and at the University of Iceland. Vigdís excelled in her academic pursuits, particularly in languages and the arts. Growing up during World War II presented hardships that influenced her outlook. Food shortages were common, and the war's impact was felt throughout Iceland (*Vigdís Finnbogadóttir*, 2020). These experiences taught her resilience and adaptability, qualities that would become essential in her life as a politician. She learned to navigate through difficult situations with grace and determination, traits that endeared her to many during her time in office.

Vigdís married Ragnar Arinbjarnar in 1954 when she was 24. They unfortunately got divorced in 1963. She focused more on her career in politics and public service after her marital status changed. Despite being divorced, she adopted her daughter in 1972 and became a single mom to Ástríður Magnúsdóttir (Pruitt, 2020). Although she experienced many challenges as a single mother, Vigdís was dedicated to raising Ástríður with strong values. She emphasized the importance of education and active participation in society. Her experiences as a mother shaped her understanding of gender equality and women's empowerment, themes she would advocate for throughout her career.

In 1980, Vigdís was elected president, a milestone that represented a major change in the landscape of political leadership. Her election demonstrated that women could achieve the highest political roles and encouraged women in Iceland and abroad (*Vigdís Finnbogadóttir*, 2020). Many began to view her victory as a beacon of hope, showing that women could challenge the traditional barriers that kept them from leadership roles. This shift empowered women and motivated them to pursue their aspirations in various fields.

Throughout her presidency, Vigdís actively worked to promote gender equality. She understood that women needed to be part of the decision-making process for real change to occur. By emphasizing the importance of women's involvement in politics, she inspired countless women to seek political representation. This was not just about filling positions; it was about ensuring that women's perspectives and experiences shaped policies that affected their lives. Her leadership opened doors for dialogue about the roles women should play in society and government. She was extremely popular as she was reelected three times, two times being unopposed and the other time winning 96% of votes. After 16 years in the presidency, her tenure was the longest of any woman elected for the presidency. Her being in office for such a long term showcased that women are more than capable of leading countries. Her dedication to Iceland, even as a single mum, can be an inspiration to us all.

She retired in 1996, but even after her presidency, Vigdís did not stop advocating for women's rights. She continued her work by representing Iceland at many international forums, including significant gatherings at the United Nations. At these events, she addressed pressing issues like violence against women, economic inequality, and barriers to education. Her presence at such forums was important, as it highlighted Iceland's commitment to gender equality on a global stage. Vigdís spoke passionately about the need for change, and her words resonated with many who were fighting for similar causes in their own countries (*Vigdís Finnbogadóttir*, 2020).

Education was another significant focus for Vigdís. She believed that empowering women through education was vital for promoting equality. Vigdís championed initiatives designed to encourage women to pursue education and engage across various sectors, such as politics, business, and science. For example, she supported scholarships for women and programs that helped them develop professional skills. By prioritizing education, she aimed to create a generation of well-informed women who could take on leadership roles in their communities.

Vigdís's leadership style was marked by her genuine dedication to social justice. She was not just a figurehead; she actively sought to improve the lives of women and children. Her approach made her a role model, showing women everywhere that they could succeed in leadership positions. Her presidency was not only about being in a high office; it was about showing that women can lead with strength and compassion.

Even after leaving office, she remained involved in social and educational causes. Vigdís worked with various organizations to continue promoting discussions around women's rights. She attended workshops, gave talks, and collaborated on projects aimed at advancing gender equality. Her efforts helped keep the conversation about women's issues alive, ensuring that progress continued beyond her presidency.

Through her dedication and efforts, Vigdís played a crucial role in changing societal attitudes toward gender roles. She challenged the norms that typically limited women's opportunities and fought for a more inclusive society. By advocating for women's rights in Iceland and internationally, she made it easier for future generations of women to follow in her footsteps and become leaders.

Vigdís's legacy is one of empowerment and inspiration. She has shown that female leadership is not only possible but also vital for a healthy society. Her impact on women's rights continues to inspire new generations of advocates and leaders every day. The work she did serves as a roadmap for those who wish to make a difference, proving that, with determination and passion, change is achievable (Hofverberg, 2020).

# Hanan Ashrawi's Efforts in Palestinian and Women's Rights

Hanan Ashrawi (1946) is an inspiring Palestinian politician, legislator, and advocate for peace and human rights, known for her significant role as a prominent spokesperson for the Palestinian cause and her efforts to promote dialogue and understanding between Israelis and Palestinians.

Hanan Ashrawi was born on October 8, 1946, in Nablus, a city located in the West Bank of Palestine. Growing up in this rich and complex environment shaped her views and aspirations significantly. As with most of the influential women we've discussed, the socio-political context of her early years provided a backdrop that influenced her future work in politics and activism. She was the youngest of five daughters, and as a child, she was surrounded by traditional Palestinian culture and family values, which directly influenced her as she formed her identity. Despite her cultural environment, she was born into a wealthy Christian family.

Hanan's father served as a distinguished physician in the British army during the Mandate period in Palestine. His profession required the family to relocate every two years to the West Bank during Hanan's early childhood. Like her father, she passionately supports Palestinian nationalism, viewing it as central to the shared identity of the Palestinian people. In the community, serving as a successful businessman and a local leader. This connection to the community instilled a sense of responsibility in her from a young age. Hanan's mother was also influential, emphasizing the importance of education. In their household, learning was a priority. The support Hanan received at home encouraged curiosity and a desire for knowledge that she carried throughout her life. This encouragement guided her through her educational journey, equipping her with the tools to navigate a world filled with challenges.

After her early schooling in Nablus, she moved to the United States for further studies. There, she attended the University of Pennsylvania, where she received a Bachelor of Arts in Literature and a Master of Arts in English Literature. In 1975, she married Emile Ashrawi, a Christian Jerusalemite, a photographer, and a theater director, and they have two daughters (*Hanan Ashrawi*, 2020). The experience of studying abroad was transformative for Hanan. It exposed her to different cultures and ideas, broadening her perspective. It was during this time that she started to understand the nuances of global politics and the importance of advocacy.

In her early years, Hanan was also deeply affected by the loss and tragedy that surrounded her life. The 1948 Arab-Israeli War and its aftermath resulted in the displacement of many Palestinian families, including her own. These events left a mark on her psyche and fueled her desire to speak out for her people. Growing up in an environment marked by struggle and resilience taught her the importance of standing up for justice. Hanan recognized that her voice could be a powerful tool to bring attention to the plight of the Palestinian people.

Because of her upbringing, Ashrawi's journey into politics was groundbreaking, particularly in representing Palestinian women—a group historically marginalized in political arenas. In her time as an activist, she has consistently emphasized the importance of having diverse voices at the table, which has helped challenge traditional gender norms and encouraged broader participation of women in governance. This representation is key to fostering a political environment that respects and incorporates the views and needs of all societal segments.

Her focus on both national liberation and gender equality struggles overlapped quite often. Advocating for both simultaneously shows us that one cannot be truly liberated without addressing the other. This approach resonates powerfully with women living in conflict zones who often face a double burden—fighting against external occupation while simultaneously battling patriarchy within their own societies. Her work inspires these women to persevere and continue advocating for their rights, imparting hope and resilience through example.

On the international stage, Ashrawi gained significant attention as a spokesperson for Palestine. Her eloquence and commitment to her cause brought Palestinian issues to global consciousness, highlighting the necessity of female representation in leadership roles. Her presence on the world stage also paved the way for a broader dialogue about the role women play in shaping peace and stability. By standing firm in international forums, Ashrawi represented her people and also became a role model for aspiring female leaders worldwide, encouraging them to engage actively in global conversations about justice and equality.

Ashrawi's story is not just about political achievements; it's about integrating women's perspectives into peacebuilding initiatives. She recognizes that sustainable peace requires the inclusion of all stakeholders, particularly those who have traditionally been sidelined. By bringing women's unique insights and experiences to the forefront of peace negotiations and reconciliation efforts, Ashrawi demonstrates that true progress is achieved through inclusivity and diversity. Her work illustrates how women's participation in such processes enriches dialogues and also enhances the effectiveness and durability of peace agreements.

Her unwavering dedication, despite numerous challenges, serves as an inspirational blueprint for future leaders. Ashrawi's resilience in the face of adversity shows us the strength needed to drive change in hostile environments. We can all learn lessons from her perseverance as a leader.

One of the critical lessons learned from Ashrawi's advocacy is the importance of strategic patience and persistence in activism. Engaging in long-term vision and meticulous planning can yield significant results over time, even in seemingly impossible circumstances. If you're striving toward social justice, adopting a similar approach of aligning goals with enduring determination can enhance your progress in driving meaningful changes in your respective areas of interest.

# Concluding Thoughts

This chapter has walked through the inspiring stories of women who have significantly contributed to the advancement of social justice. Malala Yousafzai's journey emphasizes the power of education and the courage needed to challenge oppressive systems. Her relentless dedication provided young girls with educational opportunities and also reshaped global conversations about equality and youth activism. Similarly, Wangari Maathai demonstrated the profound impact of combining environmentalism with women's rights. Her innovative approach through the Green Belt Movement empowered women by linking ecological well-being with economic sustainability, showing how local actions can drive major change.

Hanan Ashrawi's advocacy further illustrates the intersectionality between national and gender issues, reflecting the importance of diverse voices in political discourse. Her commitment to Palestinian and women's rights highlights how persistent efforts can bring about broader recognition and participation. Through their distinct efforts, these women leaders encourage current and future generations to confront injustices and work towards a more equitable society. Use these narratives as invaluable lessons of resilience, commitment, and strategic action, reminding you that your change can be a catalyst to much bigger and more significant societal transformations.

# Chapter 7:
# Voices of the LGBTQ+ Movement

In this chapter, you will be immersed in the contributions of key figures such as Marsha P. Johnson and Sylvia Rivera, both of whom played pivotal roles during the Stonewall uprising and beyond. Discover how their relentless efforts alongside initiatives like the Street Transvestite Action Revolutionaries (STAR) challenged societal norms and provided crucial support for marginalized youth. We'll also cover the world of Billie Jean King, whose strides in sports overcame gender equality and helped to break down barriers for LGBTQ+ visibility. Through examining these compelling stories, the chapter underscores the diverse strategies and personal sacrifices each leader made in their pursuit of equality, offering powerful insights into the intersectional nature of the movement. As we journey through these narratives, we uncover the profound impact these trailblazers have had on shaping conversations around rights and identity, setting the stage for today's ongoing battles for inclusivity and equal treatment.

# Marsha P. Johnson's Role in the Stonewall Uprising

Marsha P. Johnson (1945-1992) remains an influential figure in the LGBTQ+ rights movement, with her activism catalyzing important change. Marsha P. Johnson was a prominent figure in the LGBTQ+ rights movement, known for her activism and advocacy for marginalized communities. She was born Malcolm Michaels on August

24, 1945, in Elizabeth, New Jersey. Growing up in a working-class family, Marsha experienced a childhood that was challenging. As a child, she was one of many black children in a predominantly white neighborhood. This environment made her more aware of the social dynamics around her, including issues of race and class.

In her early years, Marsha faced the expectations that came with being raised in a conservative home. She attended a local public school and sometimes faced bullying due to her gender nonconformity. Despite these challenges, she remained true to herself, often exploring her identity through fashion and performance. During her childhood, she would experiment with clothing and makeup, which allowed her to express herself and find joy in her individuality.

Family life was a mix of support and struggle. Marsha had a strong connection with her mother, who taught her the importance of love and compassion. However, her relationship with her father was more complicated, filled with conflict, as he did not accept her identity. This tension shaped her understanding of acceptance and rejection, influencing her later activism. Marsha's early experiences with family would gift her with a deep sense of empathy for those who also sought acceptance in a world that often marginalized them.

When Marsha turned 18, she moved to New York City. This transition marked a significant turning point in her life. In NYC, she experienced a sense of freedom that she had not felt before. The vibrant, chaotic energy of the city offered her endless opportunities to connect with other queer individuals. It was here that she fully embraced her identity as a black transgender woman. Finding a community among the drag queens and other LGBTQ+ individuals, she began to thrive.

Marsha quickly became known in the community for her lively personality and her talent for performance art. She participated in various events, contributing to the local LGBTQ+ scene and movement. Besides her artistic endeavors, she took on the name "Marsha P. Johnson" as "P" stood for "Pay It No Mind," a phrase she would commonly use to deflect questions about her identity, embodying her philosophy of self-acceptance.

Her advocacy work started against a stark historical backdrop where societal norms repressed and marginalized many within the community. In this context, Johnson's role during the Stonewall uprising in 1969 proved invaluable. The Stonewall Uprising was a significant event in the history of LGBTQ+ rights. It took place in June 1969 in New York City at the Stonewall Inn, a gay bar located in Greenwich Village. At the time, homosexuality was largely criminalized, and LGBTQ+ individuals faced discrimination and harassment from law enforcement and society. This particular bar was one of the few places where members of the LGBTQ+ community could gather without fear of arrest, but even so, police raids were common.

On the night of June 28, 1969, police raided the Stonewall Inn. The customers in the bar were used to such raids, but this time, something was different. Instead of quietly complying with the police, the patrons decided to stand up for their rights. They fought back against the officers, and conflict began. People from the surrounding streets saw what was happening and began to join in the protest. The uprising lasted for several days, with demonstrators clashing with police. This event, often described as the spark that ignited the modern LGBTQ+ rights movement, was more than just an isolated clash; it represented a collective outcry against systemic injustice faced by LGBTQ+ individuals. The raid on the Stonewall Inn wasn't unique—bars serving LGBTQ+ patrons were routinely subjected to police raids. However, on that fateful night, Marsha P. Johnson, along with other courageous individuals, stood at the forefront, refusing to be silenced or pushed aside any longer. These moments of rebellion echo in Johnson's legacy, emphasizing the importance of her foundational activism, which has helped shape subsequent generations' fight for equality (Yang et al., 2023).

Johnson's activism did not stop at Stonewall. She went on to co-found the Street Transvestite Action Revolutionaries (STAR) with Sylvia Rivera. STAR became a lifeline for homeless transgender youth, who were often rejected by their families and society at large. Johnson's vision for STAR was rooted in addressing immediate needs—providing shelter and safety for those without homes—and a broader mission of empowerment within the LGBTQ+ community. This grassroots organization signified a new era of advocacy, one that recognized the importance of connection within the struggle for rights. It showcased the urgent need for inclusive spaces that prioritized those most often marginalized within the movement, namely transgender and gender-nonconforming people of color (Rothberg, 2022).

Culturally, Marsha P. Johnson also made valuable contributions by redefining drag culture and expression. Drag, for Johnson, was both a form of personal liberation and a bold statement against societal gender norms. She was known for her vibrant outfits and joyous parades, transforming fashion into a medium through which she could challenge and playfully subvert heteronormative expectations. In embracing drag, Johnson did more than celebrate individuality; she used her performances as a powerful tool to draw attention to LGBTQ+ issues. By being unapologetically herself, Johnson provided visibility and validation for countless others, opening doors for future artists and activists to engage with these themes openly and creatively (Ryan, 2017).

Perhaps what is most remarkable about Johnson is how her influence continues to permeate contemporary discussions around LGBTQ+ rights. In recent years, there have been growing efforts to commemorate her contributions formally. This includes initiatives like the Public Arts Campaign "She Built NYC," which commissioned a monument to honor both Marsha P. Johnson and Sylvia Rivera—the first in New York City dedicated to transgender women. Documentaries and educational programs also continue to explore her life and impact, ensuring that her story is shared with new audiences and maintaining its relevance and inspiration (Solly, 2019).

Johnson's enduring legacy is also palpable in modern movements advocating for trans rights, gay rights, and broader conversations surrounding gender identity. Her work laid the groundwork for a more inclusive and multifaceted approach to activism, teaching us that social justice must account for all voices to effect lasting change. Current dialogues around issues like healthcare access, employment non-discrimination, and legal recognition of transgender identities reflect the battles that Johnson fought throughout her life. We can integrate these elements into ongoing campaigns so that today's advocates can honor her legacy while pushing the envelope further toward true equality.

# Sylvia Rivera's Activism for Transgender Rights

Sylvia Rivera's (1951-2002) advocacy for transgender rights and inclusivity within the LGBTQ+ movement is a testament to her resilience and determination. Born in New York City in 1951, Rivera faced personal struggles from an early age that shaped her path as an activist. She has a diverse cultural background of Puerto Rican and Venezuelan descent. Her childhood was unfortunately filled with trials and challenges—abandoned by her father and losing her mother at the tender age of three. She was raised by a grandmother who struggled to accept her gender expression. By the age of eleven, Rivera had left home, thrust into a harsh world where she became both a victim of sexual exploitation and an emerging voice for change (Rothberg, 2021).

Rivera's activism truly began during the Stonewall uprising in 1969. At just 17, she found herself at the heart of what would become a pivotal moment in the fight for LGBTQ+ rights. Despite not being credited with throwing the first Molotov cocktail—an enduring myth she often dismissed—Rivera significantly contributed to those fiery nights. She stood on the front lines, challenging police oppression and supporting her fellow LGBTQ+ individuals in their struggle for recognition and equality. For Sylvia, Stonewall was more than a riot; it was a revolution—a call to arms for marginalized communities long silenced or sidelined by mainstream movements. She vividly expressed the relationship between these struggles, noting her involvement in the Black Liberation and peace movements, which further fueled her revolutionary spirit (Rothberg, 2021).

A year later, alongside Marsha P. Johnson, Rivera co-founded the Street Transvestite Action Revolutionaries (STAR). As we touched on earlier, STAR was groundbreaking—a grassroots initiative aimed at providing homeless transgender and LGBTQ+ youth with shelter, support, and community. This organization was born out of necessity, funded through the tireless efforts of its founders, who often hustled the streets to keep it afloat. STAR House, though short-lived, represented a sanctuary for those cast aside by society, offering basic security and hope to its residents. The work Rivera did with STAR was commendable as she worked toward uplifting the most vulnerable, addressing their immediate needs while advocating for broader systemic change (The History of Pride Part, n.d.).

Rivera's relentless push for inclusion extended beyond providing shelter. Her participation in the first Gay Pride March in 1970 emphasizes her fight for visibility and acknowledgment of diverse voices within the LGBTQ+ community. In 1973, when denied the chance to speak, Rivera seized the microphone to remind attendees that without drag queens and transgender individuals, there would be no gay liberation movement. Her "Y'all Better Quiet Down" speech, delivered amid boos, was a powerful plea for inclusion and recognition. It portrayed her frustration with a movement that too often prioritized the experiences of white, middle-class gays and lesbians over others. Despite the backlash, Rivera continued to stand firm, challenging the status quo and fighting for the greater representation of marginalized groups within the movement (The History of Pride Part 2, n.d.).

The impact of Sylvia Rivera's legacy is immeasurable. Her life and advocacy continue to inspire modern transgender rights activism. Through her work, Rivera brought attention to critical issues like race, gender, and economic disparities that are linked within the LGBTQ+ community. She relentlessly advocated for policies that recognized and protected the rights of transgender individuals, a fight that endures through today's ongoing battles for equality and justice. Rivera's influence persists in the continued dialogues surrounding inclusivity and the need for a comprehensive approach to LGBTQ+ rights—a movement that acknowledges and embraces the diversity of its members (Rothberg, 2021).

Reflecting on Rivera's contribution to society, it is clear that her journey was not without hardship. Throughout her life, she struggled with homelessness and substance abuse, challenges that mirrored those faced by many whom she sought to help. Despite these adversities, Rivera remained steadfast in her mission, channeling her struggles into fuel for her activism. Though she eventually stepped back from public activism, the legacy she left behind is one of courage and unwavering dedication to a cause larger than herself.

In 1997, Rivera returned to New York City and launched Transy House, a project inspired by STAR House, reaffirming her lifelong commitment to creating safe havens for transgender individuals. The enduring respect and admiration for Sylvia Rivera are evidenced by the many honors recognizing her foundational role in shaping the LGBTQ+ landscape. Whether through tangible monuments or the advancement of inclusive policies, her spirit persists, encouraging current and future activists to continue the battle for true equality.

# Billie Jean King's Fight for Equality in Sports

Billie Jean King (born in 1943) stands as a beacon of progress in the battle for gender equality and LGBTQ+ rights, particularly within the realm of sports. Billie Jean King was born on November 22, 1943, in Long Beach, California. She grew up in a typical American neighborhood during that time. Her parents, Bill and Betty Moffitt, worked hard to provide for their family. They instilled values of hard work and perseverance in Billie and her siblings. The family dynamic was supportive. King had a sister named Janet, and a brother named Randy. The Moffitt household was filled with love and encouragement, which helped shape Billie's character.

As a child, Billie faced some challenges due to the societal norms of her time. In the 1940s and 1950s, there were limited opportunities for girls, especially in sports. However, this did not deter Billie from following her passion. She started playing tennis at a young age and quickly fell in love with the game. Her family supported her enthusiasm, and they provided her with lessons and access to courts. Billie's determination and passion for tennis grew stronger as she practiced relentlessly.

Growing up in a post-World War II America, Billie Jean King experienced the cultural shifts happening around her. The country was slowly changing its views on gender roles, but traditional beliefs still held sway in many areas. While many girls were encouraged to pursue homemaking skills, Billie was encouraged to excel in sports. Her mother believed that a strong athletic background would empower her daughters. This mindset laid the foundation for Billie's emergence as a champion.

Her tennis career represents advocacy efforts, displaying resilience and determination. King's countless achievements on the court elevated her to legendary status in tennis and also provided her with a platform to fight for gender equality. With 39 Grand Slam titles under her belt, including 12 singles and numerous doubles victories ("Life Story: Billie Jean King," n.d.), she shattered stereotypes and demonstrated that women's athletic performances deserve recognition on par with men's.

King's journey toward equality is perhaps best illustrated by her role in the fight for equal pay in sports. During the early 1970s, women were consistently awarded less prize money than their male counterparts. King was undeterred by the status quo; instead, she took charge by demanding equal prize money. The climax of her efforts materialized when she famously threatened to boycott the U.S. Open in 1973 unless women received the same compensation as men. This life-changing stance resulted in the U.S. Open becoming the first major tournament to offer equal pay, setting a precedent that would ripple across professional sports (Beard, 2021).

She advocated for more than just financial equality. In 1973, King participated in the historic "Battle of the Sexes" tennis match against Bobby Riggs, a retired former Wimbledon champion who had belittled women's tennis. By defeating Riggs in front of an audience of 90 million people worldwide, King not only claimed victory in the court but also struck a symbolic blow against entrenched gender biases. This match emphasized her capability to transcend her sport to become a cultural icon advocating for women's rights.

In 1981, King's courage took another significant form when she publicly came out as a lesbian. At a time when homosexuality was heavily stigmatized, this revelation could have ended her career. However, King chose authenticity over fear, transforming what could have been a personal setback into a landmark moment for LGBTQ+ visibility in sports. Her coming out brought to light the challenges faced by LGBTQ+ individuals in athletics, prompting broader societal conversations around inclusion and acceptance (Life Story: Billie Jean King, n.d.).

Despite these personal and societal upheavals, King remained steadfast in her advocacy work. She utilized her experiences to mentor younger athletes, emphasizing the need for an inclusive sports environment where all athletes, regardless of gender or sexual orientation, are valued. Through initiatives like the Billie Jean King Leadership Initiative, she continues to push for comprehensive inclusivity and diversity both in sports and in wider society, working tirelessly to break down barriers that others might have deemed impossible to overcome.

King's influence extends beyond her public endeavors. Her legacy is enriched by various honors and recognitions that acknowledge her contributions to equality and sport. The USTA Billie Jean King National Tennis Center, home of the US Open, is named in her honor, serving as a testament to her enduring impact on the sport (Life Story: Billie Jean King, n.d.). Additionally, in 2009, King became the first female athlete to receive the Presidential Medal of Freedom, further cementing her role as a pioneer in both sports and social justice.

King's ability to bridge her tennis success with activism has left an undeniable mark on sports culture. She is a great example to many of us, as she proves how athletes can utilize their platforms to drive change, creating environments that advocate for equal opportunities and respect for all individuals. This blend of sports excellence and activism remains a powerful example for future generations.

In contemporary discussions around inclusion and equality, King's legacy persists as a guiding light. Her story inspires athletes and activists alike to strive for the equitable treatment of women and LGBTQ+ individuals in every sphere of life. By mentoring upcoming athletes and continuing to engage in dialogues around gender and sexuality, King ensures that the spirit of her advocacy lives on, encouraging new voices to rise and continue the pursuit of justice and inclusion.

# Concluding Thoughts

The chapter ventured through the powerful stories of women who have been important in advancing LGBTQ+ rights, focusing on the resilience and significant contributions of figures like Marsha P. Johnson, Sylvia Rivera, and Billie Jean King. By highlighting their relentless pursuit of justice and equality, the narrative captures the essence of their struggles and triumphs. These women's stories portray their courage and tenacity in facing societal and personal challenges. Whether standing at the forefront during the Stonewall uprising, co-founding organizations dedicated to supporting marginalized youth, or fighting for equal pay and recognition in sports, their legacies continue to inspire various movements for social justice today.

As we reflect on their enduring impact, it becomes clear that each individual's journey contributes something unique yet universally inspiring to the broader struggle for equality. Their dedication to creating inclusive spaces and pushing for systemic change emphasizes the ongoing importance of connections within activism. Whether you're seeking role models, historical context, or resources for furthering discussions on gender equality, let these narratives provide both inspiration and a framework for understanding how past battles shape present and future advocacy. The chapter reminds us that the fight for rights is not just about single acts of defiance but an accumulation of persistent efforts by those who dared to challenge the norm and envision a more equitable world.

# Chapter 8:
# Champions of Indigenous Rights

The champions of Indigenous rights also deserve acknowledgment and active support, especially the women whose leadership has had drastic impacts on cultural representation and preservation. Advocating for Indigenous rights requires acknowledgment and active support of those who have historically been underrepresented, especially women whose leadership has had significant impacts on cultural preservation and advocacy. The strength of women's roles in these movements lies in their ability to lead and also in understanding and respect for the cultural and historical context in which they operate. These leaders use their unique perspectives to develop community resilience, ensuring that Indigenous traditions and rights are not just protected but flourish amid modern challenges. Embracing this dual role of preserving and representing marginalized groups, women have proven the ability to navigate the complexities of Indigenous empowerment. This chapter discusses some of the contributions of various female figures in the arena of Indigenous rights.

# Wilma Mankiller's Leadership Within the Cherokee Nation

Wilma Mankiller (1945) is a notable leader known for being the first female chief of the Cherokee Nation, where she implemented significant social and economic reforms, advocating for Native American rights and empowerment while breaking barriers for women in leadership roles.

Wilma Mankiller was born in the 1940s, which shaped much of her early life experience. Her family hailed from the Cherokee Nation, a Native American tribe that has a rich and complex history (Roppolo,

2019). Wilma's childhood was marked by the struggles faced by many Native Americans, especially during a time when their rights and cultures were under significant pressure. Born on November 18, 1945, in Tahlequah, Oklahoma, the capital of the Cherokee Nation, Wilma was the sixth of eleven children born to Charley Mankiller and Clara Irene Sitton. The surname "Mankiller," Asgaya-dihi (Cherokee syllabary: ᎠᏍᎦᏯᏗᎯ) in the Cherokee language, refers to a traditional Cherokee military rank, like a captain or major (Brando, 2010). Growing up in a large family, Wilma often felt the weight of expectations and the importance of her heritage.

Her family moved around during her early years, which provided her with a diverse set of experiences. This mobility drastically influences the upbringing of children, encouraging them to adapt to new environments while also making them feel a sense of instability. For Wilma, this movement caused her to develop resilience. Each new place brought different challenges and opportunities to learn about herself and her people. These experiences would later contribute to the shaping of her identity and her commitment to serve her community.

Education was a significant part of Wilma Mankiller's upbringing. She attended various schools as her family moved, and she often faced discrimination as a Native American student. Her family guided her to follow a path of studies so that she could be well-educated and self-reliant. Although these experiences can be incredibly difficult, they taught her to develop a strong sense of justice. The challenges she encountered in school made her more determined to succeed and advocate for her rights and the rights of others. Wilma's early exposure to racism and inequality shaped her worldview and set the stage for her future work as a leader.

Wilma's childhood was also rich in cultural traditions that were passed down through generations. Participating in ceremonies, storytelling sessions, and family gatherings helped reinforce her connection to her Cherokee roots. These moments were more than just social gatherings; they were historical lessons that instilled a deep respect for her ancestors and their struggles. Because she learned about her culture at a young age, Wilma grew to appreciate the importance of preserving Native American heritage and traditions (Forbes, 2021).

Another component of Wilma Mankiller's childhood was her experience with role models. She was surrounded by strong figures, including her mother and grandmother, who were sources of inspiration and wisdom. These women taught her the value of perseverance and strength. Their stories of overcoming hardship became a blueprint for Wilma, showing her that it was possible to rise above challenges.

As Wilma grew older, she began to see the stark realities of life as a Native American. She witnessed the struggles of her community firsthand, including issues related to poverty, health, and education. These experiences ignited a passion for social change in her. She realized that being a voice for her people was not just an option; it was a responsibility. The lessons learned from her childhood led her to actively seek ways to improve the conditions in her community.

In her teenage years, Wilma Mankiller took on various roles that allowed her to voice her concerns and advocate for change. She participated in local organizing efforts, which helped her understand the importance of grassroots movements. This experience laid the foundation for the leadership skills she developed throughout her life. Engaging in these activities during her youth gave her a sense of purpose and clarity about her future path. Further along in her life, Wilma married from 1963 to 1977, Mankiller and had two daughters. In 1977, during their divorce, she moved back to Oklahoma with her daughters (Brando, 2010).

With all of her experiences and knowledge, Mankiller became determined with a vision for change and growth within the Cherokee Nation. She understood the importance of allowing communities to guide their futures without external interference. Under her guidance, the Cherokee Nation ventured through numerous self-determination initiatives, focusing on enhancing local governance and decision-making processes. Creating this environment where community voices were prioritized, Mankiller strengthened the tribe's autonomy and also became an inspirational model for other indigenous groups seeking similar paths toward self-governance. These initiatives emphasized the role of grassroots leadership, prompting community members to take active roles in shaping their destinies (*Wilma Mankiller*, 2024).

Mankiller's leadership led to significant improvements in health, education, and economic conditions within the Cherokee Nation. Her community development programs were detailed and easy to understand, helping people learn about the aspects of life and how advocating can result in ripple effects of change across society. An example of this was when she succeeded in the Bell Community Revitalization Project, which improved local water systems and housing, demonstrating the benefits of women-led initiatives. This project further displayed the power of women in leadership positions, as they displayed broad societal impacts that can be achieved when women are at the forefront of development efforts. Mankiller's work showed that these initiatives can uplift individual communities and also pave the way for widespread societal progress (*Wilma Mankiller,* 2009).

Along with domestic programs, Mankiller helped to advocate for legal rights and indigenous preservation. She contributed to significant legal battles that reinforced the status of the Cherokee Nation as a sovereign entity. Her work laid the groundwork for future advocacy efforts, ensuring that the quest for Indigenous rights continued beyond her leadership tenure. Mankiller's legal advocacy demonstrated that achieving sovereignty(definition for sovereignty) required persistent efforts and strategic negotiation, inspiring future generations of Indigenous leaders to persist in their fight for rights and recognition. Her perseverance and success in these legal endeavors provide guidance for Indigenous communities worldwide that are striving for representation or change (*Wilma Mankiller,* 2024).

Mankiller remained dedicated to promoting Cherokee traditions and identity as she got older. She understood that cultural heritage is not just a relic of the past but a living, vital part of sustaining indigenous identity. Mankiller worked tirelessly to revive and maintain Cherokee traditions and language, seeing them as critical elements in empowering her community and ensuring its survival despite modern challenges. Her initiatives in cultural preservation utilized educational reforms that integrated Cherokee values and history into the curriculum, creating pride and awareness among younger generations. This focus on cultural heritage emphasizes the importance of understanding your roots while navigating contemporary societal dynamics.

# Pat O'Shane's Groundbreaking Role in Australian Judiciary

Pat O'Shane (1941) is a remarkable figure recognized as the first Aboriginal woman to be elected to public office in Australia, serving as a passionate advocate for Indigenous rights, education, and social justice, and paving the way for future generations of Aboriginal leaders.

Pat O'Shane was born in 1941, the eldest of five children in Mossman, Queensland, to an Irish father and an Aboriginal mother. She grew up in an environment that shaped her values and aspirations from a young age. Growing up in a close-knit community, she was surrounded by family members who valued education and hard work. Her parents taught her to believe that anyone could achieve their dreams with determination and effort. This perspective helped her to develop the qualities she required as a justice fighter (*Pat O'Shane AM*, 2022).

From her early years, Pat was encouraged to explore her interests. She was particularly drawn to stories and the experiences of others. Her family often gathered to share tales that sparked her imagination. These storytelling sessions entertained her and also taught her valuable lessons about life, culture, and community. Through these stories, she learned about the struggles and triumphs of those around her, which helped her to develop a sense of empathy and understanding.

Pat's childhood revolved around education, marked by her achievements at a local school. Her teachers saw her promise and inspired her to chase her passions wholeheartedly. Pat developed a love for reading and writing, often losing track of time immersed in books or crafting her own tales. Her excitement for learning endeared her to both peers and teachers, who admired her readiness to support classmates in need.

Participating in community events greatly influenced Pat's perspective. She engaged in various activities led by local figures, enabling her to connect with a range of people and gain insight into the broader world. Through volunteer work, she aided those less fortunate, gaining a profound appreciation for service and the difference one individual can make. Alongside her studies, Pat embraced athletics by joining a local soccer team, enhancing her teamwork abilities, and forging friendships beyond academics. Sports instilled discipline and commitment in her, teaching her the significance of collective effort and navigating both success and defeat. The skills she honed on the field later guided her in facing life's challenges.

As she transitioned into her teenage years, Pat assumed greater responsibilities. Encouraged by her parents to engage in family decision-making, she cultivated critical thinking and independence. This involvement taught her time management, allowing her to juggle academics, extracurriculars, and family duties smoothly. These experiences laid a strong foundation for the challenges that awaited her in adulthood. Pat's upbringing was also influenced by her cultural background. She was taught to appreciate her heritage and the history of her people. Family gatherings often included discussions about past generations and their struggles. This connection to her roots was important to her development, as it provided a sense of identity and belonging. It fueled her passion to represent her culture and advocate for those who came before her.

In addition to her cultural education, Pat was exposed to various forms of art and creativity. Her parents encouraged her to express herself through music and visual arts. She took piano lessons and participated in art classes, where she learned to appreciate the beauty of creativity. These pursuits not only provided a creative outlet, but also nurtured her understanding of different perspectives and emotions.

Throughout her upbringing, Pat was fortunate to have strong role models. Her family members were not only supportive, but also ambitious. They shared stories of their own challenges and achievements, inspiring her to pursue her dreams relentlessly. These influences provided her with a framework for success and reinforced the idea that hard work pays off. Their encouragement set her on a path toward her goals and aspirations.

As she progressed through her teenage years, Pat began to develop a clearer sense of her passions and interests. She took part in various clubs and activities that aligned with her values. Joining the debate club was a turning point for her, as it allowed her to explore her views and learn how to articulate them effectively. She trained as a teacher at the Queensland Teachers' College in Brisbane, where she was the only Aboriginal woman and enrolled in a Bachelor of Education at the University of Queensland. In 1962, she married another activist, Mick Miller, and they moved to Cairns, where Pat was active in the Communist Party and Aboriginal political work. They had two daughters (*Pat O'Shane AM*, 2022).

As the first Aboriginal woman to ascend to the judiciary as a magistrate in Australia, Pat O'Shane shattered long-standing barriers within the legal profession. Her journey is more than just a personal triumph; it represents a narrative of empowerment that resonates deeply with aspiring legal professionals, particularly women of color who often face systemic challenges in the field. O'Shane's groundbreaking role serves as an inspiration, showing that despite entrenched obstacles, success is possible (Melville, 2017).

O'Shane's work extends beyond her courtroom duties. She has been an unwavering advocate for indigenous rights, actively involved in reforming policies that impact on Aboriginal communities. Her involvement in policy reform showcases her ability to guide effective lobbying methods, helping to address injustices faced by indigenous peoples. Through her efforts, significant attention was brought to inequalities embedded within the legal and social systems, proving essential in the fight for equity and justice.

Mentorship played a pivotal role in O'Shane's career. Throughout her tenure, she prioritized fostering future leaders among young Aboriginal lawyers and women in law. By offering guidance, support, and a powerful example of leadership, O'Shane significantly contributed to building a new generation of leaders who are equipped to continue advocating for Indigenous rights and representation in the legal field. This mentorship ensures that the trail she blazed will be followed by many others, thereby enhancing diversity and inclusion within the legal profession.

Public awareness of indigenous issues has been another area where O'Shane made substantial contributions. She successfully bridged the gap between the intricacies of law and the broader community activism landscape. By highlighting Indigenous stories and cultural narratives, she emphasized the importance of storytelling as a tool for education and advocacy. Her efforts have paved the way for increased visibility and understanding of Indigenous matters, engaging a wider audience in meaningful dialogue about these crucial topics.

Underpinning all of O'Shane's work is her commitment to justice and equality. Her career illustrates how powerful change can arise from courage and resilience. By breaking down stereotypes and challenging the status quo, she has carved out a legacy that extends far beyond her own accomplishments.

Community Development Initiatives, inspired by O'Shane's leadership, have demonstrated tangible improvements in health, education, and economic conditions within Indigenous communities. These programs illustrate how intentional leadership can drive sustainable change. They highlight the profound effects of women-led initiatives on societal development, showcasing that when women like O'Shane lead, they not only create opportunities for themselves but also uplift entire communities (Olsen & Lovett, 2016).

Reflecting on O'Shane's influence, it becomes clear that her pioneering role was not only about achieving personal success but also about transforming the structures around her to ensure that more voices could be heard. Her story is one of persistence, demonstrating that progress, though incremental, is achievable with dedication and strategic action.

# Irene Watson's Advocacy in Australian Politics

Irene Watson (1958) is an inspiring Aboriginal academic and activist known for her contributions to Indigenous legal studies and her advocacy for the rights of Aboriginal people in Australia, emphasizing the importance of land, culture, and identity in shaping justice and social equity.

Irene Watson grew up in a small town Coorong region and the southeast of South Australia, where everyone seemed to know each other. The sense of community was strong, and her childhood was a mix of both simplicity and warmth. In this town, Irene often played with the neighborhood kids after school. They spent hours outside, riding bikes, playing games, and exploring the nearby woods. This interaction with other children helped her to develop crucial social skills from a young age (*Trove*, 2024).

Irene came from a close-knit family and was of Aboriginal origin. Her parents were hardworking people who taught her the value of kindness. Her mother was a teacher, so learning was also highly valued in their household. Irene often saw her mother preparing lessons, and this inspired her to appreciate knowledge and the joy of learning. Because they were a close-knit family, having family dinners was a common occurrence, where they would sit together to share stories about their day. This practice brought them closer and created open conversations about various topics, allowing Irene to express her thoughts freely.

In school, Irene was eager to learn. She had a curious mind and often asked questions, wanting to know more about the world around her. This curiosity led her to excel in her studies. Her teachers noticed her enthusiasm and often encouraged her to participate in class discussions. For example, when the class was learning about science, Irene would often volunteer to conduct experiments. This hands-on experience made the learning process enjoyable for her and helped solidify her understanding of different subjects.

Like many children, Irene faced challenges during her upbringing. There were times when she struggled with self-doubt, especially during adolescence. As she worked through the complexities of growing up, she sometimes felt pressure to fit in with her peers. However, her family's support helped her overcome these feelings. They encouraged her to stay true to herself and embrace her uniqueness. Through open discussions and reassurance, Irene learned the importance of self-acceptance and resilience.

Irene Watson was the first Aboriginal person to graduate from the University of Adelaide with a law degree in 1985. She was also the first Aboriginal PhD graduate (2000) at the university, winning the

Bonython Law Prize for the best thesis. Watson is a prominent figure in the landscape of political reform and advocacy for indigenous rights in Australia. Her journey reveals the significant impact that engaged and meaningful leadership can have on advocating for policy changes, particularly those affecting Indigenous communities. Recognizing the deep-seated issues faced by these communities, Watson used her influence to spotlight and address issues in education and health care that had long been neglected (*Trove*, 2024).

Watson's rise to political prominence did not happen overnight. It was the result of years of dedication to social justice and equality, driven by personal experiences and an undying commitment to her community. In an environment historically resistant to change, Watson emerged as a beacon of hope, showcasing that persistent and informed engagement could drive substantive policy shifts. Her advocacy efforts emphasized the need for leaders who understood the intricacies of the challenges indigenous communities faced, but also had the resolve and capability to challenge the status quo.

Her initiatives were groundbreaking, especially in addressing inequality within Indigenous education and health systems, areas that had suffered from systemic neglect. By focusing on these forms, Watson exposed practical methods for systemic change, rallying for policies that would ensure better educational outcomes and healthcare access for Indigenous peoples. These efforts contributed to bridging the significant gaps in these sectors and brought them to the forefront of national discourse, thus setting a precedent for future leaders and advocates.

A key strategy in Watson's advocacy was her ability to build coalitions, working alongside various organizations and stakeholders to spread her cause. This advocacy represented the power of coalition-building in creating community support and enhancing the reach and impact of fighting for change. Uniting diverse voices and expertise enabled Watson to craft compelling arguments that aligned with policymakers and the general public. This reaffirmed the idea that collective action is often more powerful than isolated efforts.

Watson recognized the importance of empowering the next generation of indigenous leaders. Her youth empowerment initiatives were designed to nurture young Indigenous talent, providing them with the tools and opportunities needed to develop their leadership skills. Watson addressed the immediate community needs and lay the foundation for long-term leadership among indigenous Australians by investing in the youth. These initiatives emphasized leadership development, encouraging young people to take pride in their heritage by effectively integrating.

One of Watson's most notable contributions was her role in major research projects that influenced policy-making. Her work on Aboriginal and Islander child welfare in Queensland, for instance, provided critical data that informed the creation of the Child Protection Act of 1999. This legislative achievement showcased how research and empirical evidence could be harnessed to bring about meaningful change, further cementing Watson's legacy as a trailblazer in Indigenous advocacy.

Beyond her political and social endeavors, Watson also embraced roles in various boards and institutions, including the Queensland Parole Board and the University of Queensland Senate. Her involvement in these positions allowed her to advocate for Indigenous perspectives at broader institutional levels, ensuring that Indigenous voices were heard in decisions that affected their lives directly.

Watson's life's work extends into academia and art, where she has continued to make significant impacts. As a visual artist, she has used innovative techniques to explore themes of spirituality, cultural identity, and connection to land, with her artwork receiving both national and international acclaim. This creative expression complements her advocacy work, offering another platform to educate and inspire others about Indigenous culture and history (*Teachers Notes*, n.d.).

# Tunisian Women's Activism During the Arab Spring

In the heart of the Arab Spring, from December 2010, Tunisian women emerged as formidable agents of change, championing democracy and social justice (*What Is the Arab Spring, and How Did It Start?*, 2020). Their role in this historic movement cannot be overstated, as they led protests, organized communities, and catalyzed deep societal transformations. These actions highlighted the power of collective effort in driving major social upheavals.

Tunisian women were pivotal in igniting the flame of revolution. During the Jasmine Revolution, the self-immolation of Mohamed Bouazizi on December 17, 2010, became a symbol of widespread poverty and repression, but it was the persistent mobilization by women that truly fanned the flames of protest. Women from diverse backgrounds took to the streets, embodying the spirit of resistance. As professors, students, and ordinary citizens, they stood shoulder to shoulder with men, demanding political reform and an end to tyranny. Their resilience and courage exemplified the impact of grassroots movements in propelling societal shifts and demonstrated that when communities unite, they possess the strength to dismantle oppressive regimes.

A key aspect of their activism was advocating for gender equality in the new political landscape formed post-revolution. The transitional government introduced laws mandating female representation in legislative bodies, thanks largely to the relentless efforts of women's civil society groups. This fight for representation underscored the broader global struggle for gender rights, with Tunisia becoming a focal point. Despite barriers, such as parties placing women low on electoral lists, many rose to positions of influence. They defied traditional gender roles, proving that women's participation is vital in shaping progressive governance (The Arab Spring and Women's Rights in Tunisia, 2013).

Beyond mere representation, Tunisian women were instrumental in promoting human rights and cultural expression during these tumultuous times. The revolution sparked a profound dialogue about identity and freedom, and women placed themselves at the forefront of this conversation. They advocated for cultural and artistic expressions that reinforced the importance of preserving Tunisian identity amidst chaos. By doing so, they preserved a sense of dignity and continuity that energized the population's aspiration for democratic ideals (Carter, 2022).

Education emerged as both a tool and a testament to Tunisian women's strategic vision for future empowerment. Recognizing that knowledge prevails where repression fails, they invested heavily in educational initiatives. Various programs aimed at enhancing literacy and providing vocational training were launched to bridge gaps left by the previous regime. These initiatives not only equipped young generations with critical skills but also instilled a sense of agency among the youth, empowering them to envision and realize their potential contributions to society's advancement.

In educational settings, discussions about gender disparities and human rights became integral, creating an environment of critical thinking. Female educators played crucial roles in reshaping curricula to include perspectives on feminist theory and civic duty. Such measures encouraged young girls, who had long been marginalized, to aspire beyond conventional domestic roles. They were taught to see themselves as leaders, thinkers, and innovators capable of contributing to societal progress.

The Jasmine Revolution served as a crucible from which emerged new ideas and aspirations. Women's continuous presence at the core of this movement laid the groundwork for other democratic aspirations across the Arab world. Tunisia's transition, spearheaded and sustained by women's tireless efforts, inspired similar pursuits for freedom and equity in neighboring countries. It set a precedent for how women's activism can fundamentally alter the socio-political fabric of nations.

These endeavors highlight that the quest for democracy and social justice is inexorably linked with gender equality. The Tunisian example illustrates how women's involvement enhances the robustness and inclusivity of any movement seeking transformative societal change. As trailblazers during the Arab Spring, Tunisian women showed that true emancipation is a collaborative journey, inherently enriched by the determination and voices of all its people.

# Final Insights

In the chapter, we took a look at the invaluable contributions of women like Wilma Mankiller, Pat O'Shane, Tunisian activists, and Irene Watson. These inspirational figures advocated for gender equality and their own indigenous rights. These women broke barriers and represented their communities, striving for cultural preservation. Through grassroots leadership, legal advocacy, and educational reforms, they demonstrated an ongoing commitment to uplifting marginalized voices and preserving cultural identity. Their stories emphasize the importance of women in leadership positions and how they can drive societal progress through collective empowerment and strategic action.

As we reflect on their achievements, it's evident that these women's efforts have set powerful examples for future generations to follow. They have shown that with resilience and dedication, women can lead impactful movements that transform societies. The stories in this chapter can be inspiring to us all, reminding us that we are all united in shaping history by encouraging female leadership and celebrating women from different cultures.

# Chapter 9:
# Environmental Advocates: Protecting Our Planet

Environmental advocates work diligently to safeguard our planet for future generations. This chapter discusses the lives and achievements of remarkable women who have led significant environmental movements around the world. These women fight for both ecological preservation and also for gender equality. By shining a light on their accomplishments, this chapter can inspire us to recognize and embrace the transformative power that comes from achieving social justice when addressing pressing environmental issues. As each story unfolds, the impact of these amazing women showcases how they've contributed to environmental change. Through this chapter we will explore the journeys of influential figures like Greta Thunberg, Wangari Maathai, and Rachel Maddow, each contributing uniquely to environmental advocacy.

# Greta Thunberg's Youth-Led Climate Movement

In the current age of climate discourse, young voices are becoming the dynamic forces for change, reshaping environmental activism and inspiring a new generation to advocate for climate action. At the foundation of this movement is Greta Thunberg, whose initiative, "Fridays for Future," has not only drawn international attention to critical climate issues but has also empowered youth across the globe to take an active role in advocating for a sustainable future. She is a trailblazing climate activist recognized for her relentless efforts to raise global awareness about climate change.

Greta Thunberg was born on January 3, 2003, in Stockholm, Sweden. Growing up in a city filled with beautiful parks and access to nature, Greta had the opportunity to explore her surroundings and develop a love for the environment. Her family played a significant role in shaping her values. Her father, Svante Thunberg, is an actor, and her mother, Malena Ernman, is an opera singer. Both parents were deeply engaged in environmental issues, influencing Greta from a young age. This environment inspired her to care about the world around her.

From an early age, Greta exhibited signs of a determined and thoughtful child. When she was just eight years old, she learned about climate change in school. The information made a profound impact on her. She began to understand the dangers that climate change posed to the planet. It was not just a scientific topic for Greta; it became a source of concern for her. This knowledge ignited a fire within her, leading her to question why more people were not taking action to combat climate change.

Greta's childhood was not just marked by her environmental activism. She also faced personal challenges that shaped her identity. She was diagnosed with Asperger's syndrome, obsessive-compulsive disorder, and selective mutism. These conditions made social interactions difficult for her. However, Greta turned these challenges into strengths. Her obsessive nature of details helped her dive deep into research about environmental issues. Instead of viewing her selective mutism as a limitation, she found a powerful voice through her writings and speeches.

As she navigated her childhood, Greta's passion for the environment grew stronger. She began to speak out about climate issues at school and participated in various projects to create awareness among her peers. She organized small events that encouraged her classmates to think about sustainability. This included activities like recycling drives, tree planting, and educational workshops. Greta's determination to educate those around her showcased her ability to lead from a young age.

Greta Thunberg's journey began with a singular act of protest that rapidly evolved into a global phenomenon. In August 2018, at just 15 years old, Thunberg decided to skip school every Friday to sit outside the Swedish parliament, holding a sign that read "Skolstrejk för klimatet" (School strike for climate). Her message was simple yet profound: the climate crisis demanded immediate and serious attention from political leaders. This solitary stand resonated deeply with young people around the world, leading to the birth of the 'Fridays for Future' movement (Fridays For Future, 2024).

The impact of Thunberg's movement has been vast and transformative. What began as a small protest in Sweden quickly mushroomed into a worldwide call to action, sparking climate strikes in more than 7,500 cities and engaging millions of participants globally. Through the power of social media, Thunberg leveraged platforms like Instagram and Twitter to spread her message, mobilize support, and create a sense of urgency that transcends borders. This digital mobilization has allowed her to reach a massive audience, including those who might not have previously engaged with environmental issues (Fridays For Future, 2024).

Despite her success in galvanizing a global youth movement, Thunberg has faced considerable criticism and skepticism from various political leaders who often dismissed her efforts as naive or overly simplistic. Yet, her resilience amidst such challenges underscores a powerful theme: determination in the face of adversity. Thunberg's unwavering commitment to her cause has not only encouraged ongoing advocacy but has also highlighted the importance of listening to youthful perspectives in discussions about climate policy (UNICEF, 2023).

Greta Thunberg represents a significant shift in how society perceives climate action. Her unyielding focus on the urgency of the crisis has brought climate change to the forefront of a global conversation, challenging older generations to reevaluate their environmental policies and practices. This shift is particularly important as it increases youth involvement in environmental activism, ensuring that their voices are heard in debates that will shape their futures.

Beyond individual initiatives, the impact of Thunberg's movement can be seen in the way it has inspired other young activists worldwide. Figures like María from Mexico, who became a full-time climate activist due to the severe water crisis in her region, demonstrate how Thunberg's influence extends far beyond Europe. María uses her platform to emphasize the interconnectedness of environmental issues, rallying for forest preservation as a means to tackle water scarcity (UNICEF, 2023).

Similarly, Russell Raymond from Dominica harnesses his experiences from Hurricane Maria to chronicle the hurricane's impact through photography, spotlighting the urgent need for renewable energy sources like solar and wind power. His storytelling serves to personalize the climate narrative, making abstract numbers and statistics relatable through lived experiences (UNICEF, 2023).

Another remarkable voice is that of Mitzi Jonelle Tan from the Philippines, whose activism during the COVID-19 pandemic highlights the intersection of climate justice and community welfare. As back-to-back hurricanes ravaged her country, she and her organization provided aid while gathering stories from affected communities to demand accountability and drive systemic change. Her work underscores the broader implications of climate action as a form of seeking justice (UNICEF, 2023).

Lastly, Nkosilathi Nyathi from Zimbabwe exemplifies the proactive stance taken by today's youth. Witnessing firsthand the visible changes wrought by climate change, he advocates for greater awareness and education, urging his peers to engage actively rather than remain passive observers. His message resonates with Thunberg's call to action: there is no better time to act than now (UNICEF, 2023).

These young activists collectively symbolize the burgeoning wave of youth-led environmental advocacy, echoing Thunberg's sentiments and expanding the dialogue to include diverse global perspectives. They serve as tangible evidence of Thunberg's key legacy: awakening a generation to the reality of climate change and the necessity of action.

By standing resolute against criticism and maintaining a clear focus on climate action, Thunberg and her peers exemplify the potential of young voices to drive substantive change. Their stories inspire others to join the movement, fostering a culture of environmental consciousness that bridges generational divides. As these young leaders continue to challenge norms and advocate for sustainable futures, they remind us all of the power of relentless dedication and the incredible impact youth can have in shaping a better world for everyone.

# Wangari Maathai's Green Belt Movement in Africa

Wangari Maathai (1940-2011) was an amazing environmentalist and political activist known for founding the Green Belt Movement in Kenya, which focused on tree planting, environmental conservation, and women's empowerment, making her the first African woman to receive the Nobel Peace Prize in 2004 for her contributions to sustainable development and human rights.

Wangari Maathai was born on April 1, 1940, in the small village of Ikolomani in Kenya. Her parents, who were both farmers, provided a simple but nurturing environment for her early years. Growing up in a rural community, she experienced life closely tied to the land. Her family relied on farming to survive, which gave her a deep appreciation for nature from an early age. The lush landscapes of Kenya and the beauty of the countryside had a significant impact on her.

She experienced both highs and lows in her relationships, which shaped her views and her activism. Maathai was married to Mwangi Maathai in 1960, and the two had three children together. In the early years of their marriage, they shared a strong bond. However, over time, their relationship became strained. Wangari faced many challenges during her marriage. Mwangi often struggled with her growing independence and her public life. As she became more involved in activism and politics, the dynamics in their relationship shifted. Wangari was passionate about her work, particularly through the Green Belt Movement, which focused on environmental conservation and women's rights. This dedication took a toll on her marriage. The couple eventually separated in 1977.

During her childhood, Wangari was curious and eager to learn. Her parents valued education, and they made sacrifices to ensure she could go to school. While many girls at the time were expected to stay at home and assist with household chores, Wangari's family encouraged her to pursue her studies. This commitment to education became a cornerstone of her upbringing. She attended her primary school in the local area, where she quickly stood out due to her intelligence and desire to learn.

After completing her primary education, Wangari moved to the city of Nairobi for secondary school. This transition was significant, as it brought new challenges and opportunities. Nairobi was a bustling urban center, quite different from life in Ikolomani. The culture shock was profound, but it opened her eyes to new ideas and ways of thinking. In Nairobi, she continued to excel academically and was recognized for her leadership skills. Wangari joined a local group that advocated for students' rights, showcasing her early ability to advocate for change.

While studying in the United States, Wangari also encountered other cultures and ideas about social justice. She became aware of the struggles faced by people around the world. This awareness fueled her passion for activism and instilled in her the importance of giving back to her community. Wangari was deeply influenced by the civil rights movements and women's movements occurring at the same time. This experience inspired her to fight for the rights of women and the environment back home in Kenya.

Returning to Kenya after her studies in the United States was both exciting and daunting for Wangari. She found herself eager to apply her knowledge, but also faced the reality of a changing Kenya. The political landscape was shifting, and issues like deforestation, land use, and social inequality were rising to the forefront. She began her journey in activism by focusing on environmental issues. Wangari recognized that many local communities relied on natural resources for their livelihoods. She understood that preserving these resources was essential for both the environment and the people.

Wangari Maathai, a pioneering environmental activist, founded the Green Belt Movement in 1977 to address urgent environmental concerns while empowering women. Under her leadership, this movement became a powerful force for ecological conservation and social change, highlighting the intrinsic link between women's rights and environmental integrity.

Maathai's journey began with an acute awareness of the challenges faced by rural Kenyan women. These women often reported shrinking water sources, diminishing food supplies, and the arduous task of walking long distances to gather firewood. Recognizing these struggles as symptoms of widespread environmental degradation, Maathai initiated a grassroots movement focused on tree planting—a simple yet profound solution.

The Green Belt Movement has since planted over 50 million trees across Kenya, transforming landscapes and communities. This mass reforestation effort has not only restored ecosystems but also bolstered the livelihoods of countless individuals. By rejuvenating deforested areas, the initiative has helped stabilize local climates, ensuring more consistent rainfall patterns and preserving biodiversity. Tree planting acts as a natural bulwark against soil erosion, safeguarding agricultural lands and increasing their productivity. This underscores the importance of sustainable practices in fostering both environmental and economic resilience within local communities.

A guiding principle of the Green Belt Movement is its focus on education and training, particularly for women. Maathai recognized that equipping women with the knowledge to manage natural resources was key to sustainable development. The movement offers training programs on tree nursery establishment, sustainable land use, and climate adaptation strategies. By empowering women with these skills, the movement not only nurtures environmental stewards but also enhances gender equity—both crucial components for long-term ecological health.

Educating women in resource management brings numerous benefits. It builds community leadership and fosters independence, enabling women to make informed decisions regarding land and resources. Furthermore, educating women can lead to healthier families and communities, as they are more likely to invest in their children's education and well-being when economically empowered. This creates a positive feedback loop where environmental stewardship and gender equality feed into each other, advancing both social and ecological objectives.

The impact of the Green Belt Movement extends beyond Kenya, aligning with global environmental goals and emphasizing the interconnectedness of gender equity and climate action. Wangari Maathai's initiative reflects international efforts like the United Nations' Sustainable Development Goals, which advocate for gender equality (Goal 5) and climate action (Goal 13). Her work serves as a poignant example of how grassroots initiatives can contribute to these targets, demonstrating that local actions can resonate globally.

Furthermore, Maathai's dedication was instrumental in reshaping perceptions about the role of women in environmental advocacy. Traditionally, women have been underrepresented in decision-making positions within the environmental sector. However, Maathai broke barriers, inspiring a new generation of female leaders who understand the vital connections between environmental conservation and women's empowerment.

The broader significance of Maathai's work lies in its ability to galvanize a diverse range of stakeholders—from local communities to international policymakers—around a common cause. Her efforts showcase the power of inclusive leadership and collaborative action in addressing complex global challenges. As the effects of climate change become increasingly pronounced, such integrated approaches are essential for building resilient societies capable of navigating future uncertainties.

## Rachel Maddow's Journalistic Focus on Environmental Issues

Rachel Maddow (1973) is an inspiring political commentator and television host known for her insightful analysis and progressive perspective on current events, making her one of the most influential figures in American media through her Emmy Award-winning program, "The Rachel Maddow Show."

Rachel Maddow was born on April 1, 1973, in Castro Valley, California. She grew up in a middle-class family with one brother and was raised in a supportive environment (*Family Tree of Rachel Maddow*, n.d.). Her parents, who were both educators, instilled the value of learning from an early age. This emphasis on education played a significant role in shaping her character and aspirations.

Maddow's mother was a schoolteacher, and her father worked as a former Air Force captain. Growing up in a household where discussions about current events and politics were common influenced her early interests. The family often engaged in conversations that encouraged critical thinking. This environment motivated Maddow to be curious about the world around her. She became an avid reader, diving into books that covered various subjects, including history and politics.

During her childhood, Rachel attended elementary and middle school in Castro Valley. She was known as a bright student who excelled in her studies. Maddow participated in diverse extracurricular activities, contributing to her development. For example, she joined the debate team, where she honed her skills in argumentation and public speaking. This experience would later prove invaluable in her career as a television host and political commentator.

In high school, she attended Castro Valley High School, where she continued to showcase her academic abilities. She was involved in student government and other leadership roles. These experiences solidified her confidence and provided her with a platform to express her opinions. Maddow's peers recognized her as a passionate advocate for various causes, exposing her to the early stages of public service.

Maddow's family values also played a crucial role in her upbringing. Her parents taught her the importance of social justice and equality. They encouraged her to be compassionate and understand the struggles of others. This foundational belief helped shape her perspective and commitment to addressing societal issues throughout her career.

Rachel's family was supportive of her decision to pursue higher education. After high school, she attended Smith College, where she majored in political science. Smith College, a historically women's college in Northampton, Massachusetts, offered her an enriching academic environment. During her college years, she further developed her passion for politics and journalism.

While in college, Rachel participated in various activities, such as writing for the college newspaper. Here, she found her voice as a writer and commentator. Her work covered a range of issues, from local politics to national events, laying the groundwork for her future career. Rachel also interned at several organizations, gaining valuable experience in the fields of journalism and public policy.

After completing her undergraduate degree, Maddow pursued graduate studies at Oxford University as a Rhodes Scholar. This opportunity allowed her to deepen her knowledge of politics and international relations. She focused on topics that mattered to her, such as power dynamics and the role of media in society. This academic journey helped refine her analytical skills and critical thinking.

Throughout her upbringing and education, Maddow faced challenges, including navigating her identity as a lesbian. She embraced her sexual orientation while in college, which was an important and formative experience. This aspect of her life has influenced her work in advocating for LGBTQ+ rights and representation in media. By openly discussing her experiences, she has helped raise awareness of issues affecting the LGBTQ+ community.

Maddow's childhood experiences and educational background prepared her for a career in journalism. The values instilled in her by her parents, combined with her academic pursuits, fostered a strong sense of justice. These elements combined to shape her approach to broadcasting. After finishing her studies, she began her career in radio. Rachel's early experiences helped her develop a distinct voice, characterized by her insightful analysis and engaging storytelling. Her background in debate and writing allowed her to present complex topics in a way that resonates with a broad audience.

As Maddow transitioned to television, she gained prominence for her unique style and ability to break down intricate political matters. Her successes can be traced back to her formative years, where her upbringing and experiences laid the foundation for her future achievements. Maddow created a platform where important issues could be discussed and debated, helping to inform and educate viewers.

Rachel Maddow stands as a testament to the power of journalism in amplifying environmental issues and fueling public discourse. Her platform uniquely highlights how politics intertwine with environmentalism, offering audiences crucial insights into complex topics that impact our world. The way she weaves these narratives allows her viewers to connect political maneuvers directly to their environmental consequences, stimulating thoughtful debate and pushing for accountability.

One significant element of Maddow's work is her investigation into environmental policies and corporate accountability. She dives deep into the motivations behind political decisions, often unveiling hidden aspects of policymaking that affect ecological well-being. Her approach is to lay bare the connections between what's happening in boardrooms, government offices and the resulting environmental repercussions. For instance, by dissecting the relationship between oil corporations and political regimes, Maddow brings clarity on how such interactions can shape national and international agendas (Drugmand, 2019).

In her storytelling, Maddow not only presents facts but also crafts a rich narrative that fosters a deeper understanding of what's at stake. This method is essential in engaging viewers at a level that transcends mere information dissemination. Storytelling becomes a tool for empathy and connection, inviting her audience to see the issues through lenses of justice and equity. It's about more than just environmental degradation; it's about who is affected and why their voices matter. This focus on the human side of environmental issues elevates public consciousness, urging individuals to consider implications beyond statistics and reports.

Maddow's coverage is adept at mobilizing public sentiment, showcasing journalism's potential to shift opinions and promote active stances toward sustainability. When audiences are informed and emotionally engaged, they are more likely to take action, whether it's through supporting specific policies, advocating for change, or altering personal habits. Public pressure, driven by knowledgeable citizens, becomes a powerful force in steering sustainable governance.

The intersection of media coverage and environmental advocacy underlines the need for transparency and education in empowering society. By shedding light on environmental stakes, journalists like Maddow play an integral role in democratizing knowledge, ensuring that critical information reaches broad audiences and prompts widespread engagement. She elucidates how the media can act as a check against unchecked corporate power and politically motivated environmental negligence (Benen, 2015).

In addition, Maddow's investigations serve as templates for how journalism should address environmental topics—thoroughly, passionately, and responsibly. Her ability to link intricate political strategies to their broader ecological impacts exemplifies the transformative capacity of investigative journalism. It's not merely about reporting events but about revealing patterns, predicting outcomes, and driving introspective discussions that challenge the status quo. She has won multiple accolades for her work, including the Walter Cronkite Faith & Freedom Award and a GLAAD Media Award for her coverage of LGBTQ issues. (*Rachel Maddow*, 2024).

Viewers regularly see how Maddow connects the dots between environmental events and their societal catalysts, effectively encouraging a culture of inquiry and skepticism. By doing so, she empowers her audience to demand greater transparency and responsibility from those in power. Journalism thus becomes an educational force, equipping people with the knowledge necessary to participate in meaningful dialogues about our planet's future.

Moreover, Maddow's influence demonstrates the latent potential within media to champion sustainable practices. Through consistent coverage of environmental topics, journalists can maintain focus on what requires immediate attention, therefore embedding sustainability into everyday conversations. Such continued emphasis helps prevent issues from being sidelined amid other pressing global matters.

# Summary and Reflections

This chapter discussed the significant influence women have on environmental movements. Their commitment to creating a healthier planet for future generations can inspire us all to be more environmentally friendly. Through the stories of figures like Greta Thunberg and Wangari Maathai, we see how individual dedication can make a notable contribution by transforming into global initiatives. Thunberg's 'Fridays for Future' is just one example of the modern wave of youth activism, revealing the powerful impact that young voices can have in shaping climate discussions. Her narrative can encourage countless others to join the fight against climate change. On the other hand, Wangari Maathai's Green Belt Movement demonstrates the enduring link between women's empowerment and sustainable development. Empowering women through education and resource management aids environmental preservation and also propels gender equality forward.

These remarkable stories carry broader implications, highlighting the interconnectedness of gender equality with environmental advocacy. The work of these women illustrates how grassroots initiatives can influence global agendas, spurring progress toward international goals like sustainable development and climate action. Each initiative showcases diverse methods of addressing ecological issues while elevating women's roles as leaders and change-makers. Their collective efforts inspire audiences, whether seeking role models, understanding feminism, or engaging in social justice dialogues. This chapter reinforces the idea that meaningful change often begins with determined individuals who dare to challenge norms, offering hope for a more equitable and sustainable world.

# Conclusion

Throughout this journey of exploring the inspiring stories of women who have shaped history, we've learned about the resilience and courage that can bind past struggles with future aspirations. As we navigated their stories, our understanding of feminism deepened through the connected nature of equality, justice, and empowerment. The lives of these remarkable figures—Mary Wollstonecraft, Malala Yousafzai, Susan B. Anthony, Rosa Parks, Greta Thunberg, and Wangari Maathai—are powerful reminders that the fight for women's rights transcends generations and geographical boundaries.

This book emphasizes an enduring truth: women's relentless advocacy and spirit have always been valuable in encouraging conversations about social justice. From the era of Susan B. Anthony and her campaign for women's suffrage to Rosa Parks' steadfast stand against racial segregation, historical milestones show how past struggles have paved the way for current disagreements and struggles on gender equality. These influential efforts now form the foundation for contemporary conversations around inclusion and diversity, creating a continuum where each battle shapes the next.

The evolution of feminism is beautifully complex, filled with significant achievements and ongoing challenges. Despite challenges and adversity, the consistent determination of women worldwide from all decades and centuries creates a world where equal rights and opportunities are realities rather than distant dreams. This movement is not just historical; it is alive, dynamic, and continually evolving, thanks to voices like Malala's, speaking boldly for girls' education, and Greta Thunberg's, rallying young people to protect our planet. Their contributions remind us that feminism is not static but an ever-growing force that adapts to meet new societal challenges as they emerge.

We have also explored the necessity of embracing a more connected lens within feminism—a perspective that recognizes the diverse identities and experiences shaping women's lives globally. Effective advocacy requires acknowledging the relationship between race, class, sexuality, and cultural backgrounds and recognizing that true empowerment demands this inclusivity. Across various timelines and contexts, the collective strength of women comes from honoring these differences while uniting under the broader call for equality. Acknowledging this connection ensures that no voice is marginalized, and no experience overlooked, thus enriching the feminist narrative and movement, strengthening its impact across all aspects of society.

As the torch is passed to future generations, let us envision a world where young girls, inspired by the heroines discussed in this book, dare to dream grandly and act boldly. Imagine the ripple effects if today's youth took inspiration from individuals like Wangari Maathai, achieving environmental activism, or Malala Yousafzai, advocating for girls' education, to ignite change within their communities. This sense of legacy, where one generation builds upon the achievements of another, is essential for sustaining momentum in feminist movements. These narratives encourage others to continue working against discrimination and inequality, contributing to more meaningful change.

While much attention is given to prominent figures whose activism has captured global awareness, let us not forget the unsung heroines whose stories remain largely untold. Within the realm of feminism and social justice, countless women have tirelessly worked behind the scenes, making significant yet often overlooked contributions. Their quiet strength and persistence deserve recognition alongside the celebrated icons we know. By broadening our understanding of impactful figures, we create space for these remarkable women, acknowledging their invaluable contributions and ensuring that their legacies inspire future activists.

As we close off these many inspiring stories, we can feel renewed with understanding and motivation. Let these narratives inspire you to further feminist movements by voicing your perspectives on gender equality, environmental stewardship, and social justice. Each story we've journeyed through displays the power of collective action and the difference you make when we unite under shared values. This message is relevant and valuable to us today, as much as it was in the early days of the suffrage movement.

Embrace the lessons and inspirations shared within these pages so that you can feel empowered to contribute to positive change by using the wisdom you've learned from past leaders while adding a fresh perspective from your unique experience.

Let this book be a reminder that feminism is a broad movement that belongs to everyone willing to challenge discrimination and work towards a better tomorrow. The narrative for feminism is ever-evolving and changing, filled with courage, conviction, and compassion. As you move forward, cherish the stories of those who have paved the way while also committing to forging new paths that elevate and empower all women everywhere.

# References

"The way of progress was neither swift nor easy." (2018, February 1). *AM.* https://www.amdigital.co.uk/insights/blog/taking-a-closer-look-at-the-legacy-left-by-marie-curie

*19th Amendment to the U.S. constitution: Women's right to vote (1920).* (2022, February 8). National Archives. https://www.archives.gov/milestone-documents/19th-amendment

*7 Unsung heroines who changed the course of history.* (n.d.). MSNBC.com. https://www.msnbc.com/know-your-value/7-unsung-heroines-who-changed-course-history-n1259314

*Ada Lovelace's legacy: inspired and inspiring* (2016, August 4). Earlham Institute. https://www.earlham.ac.uk/articles/ada-lovelaces-legacy-inspired-and-inspiring

Alkassim, S. (2016, April 20). *Conversation with Hanan Ashrawi: Reflections on Palestinian politics and society.* The Jerusalem Fund. https://thejerusalemfund.org/2016/04/conversation-hanan-ashrawi-reflections-palestinian-politics-society/

Barkdull, C. (2009, May). Exploring intersections of identity with native American women leaders. *Affilia.* https://doi.org/10.1177/0886109909331700

Basia Grodyńska. (2023, September 28). *Maria Skłodowska-Curie: A Catalyst for women in STEM.* The Average Scientist. https://theaveragescientist.co.uk/2023/09/28/maria-sklodowska-curie-a-catalyst-for-women-in-stem/

Beard, A. (2021, September 1). *Life's work: An Interview with Billie Jean King.* Harvard Business Review. https://hbr.org/2021/09/lifes-work-an-interview-with-billie-jean-king

Benen, S. (2015, December 17). *EPA "propaganda" isn't quite as dramatic as advertised.* MSNBC.com; MSNBC. https://www.msnbc.com/rachel-maddow-show/epa-propaganda-isnt-quite-dramatic-advertised-msna755346

Bestmann, R. (2018). *A Vindication of the rights of woman (1792) by Mary Wollstonecraft | Towards Emancipation?* Hist259.Web.unc.edu. https://hist259.web.unc.edu/vindicationofrightsofwomen/

Bhardwaj, G. (2019, November 6). *Julia Gillard on breaking barriers for women in politics.* Www.chathamhouse.org. https://www.chathamhouse.org/2019/11/julia-gillard-breaking-barriers-women-politics

Billups, S., Thelamour, B., Thibodeau, P., & Durgin, F. H. (2022, November 26). On intersectionality: visualizing the invisibility of Black women. *Cognitive Research: Principles and Implications.* https://doi.org/10.1186/s41235-022-00450-1

Brando, E. (2010). *Wilma Mankiller.* National Women's History Museum. https://www.womenshistory.org/education-resources/biographies/wilma-mankiller

Brellan, K. (2019, August 31). *Vigdis finnbogadóttir: The world's first female president | amazing women in history.* Amazing Women in History. https://amazingwomeninhistory.com/vigdis-finnbogadottir-worlds-first-female-president/

Burnette, C. E., & Figley, C. R. (2016, November 5). *Historical oppression, resilience, and transcendence: Can a holistic framework help explain violence experienced by Indigenous people?* Social Work. https://doi.org/10.1093/sw/sww065

Carter, A. (2022, June 7). *Women In the Arab spring uprisings: Tunisia - Orion policy institute.* Orion Policy Institute. https://orionpolicy.org/women-in-the-arab-spring-uprisings-tunisia/

*Celebrating Ada Lovelace as a woman in tech.* (2018, October 9). Women in Technology. https://www.womenintech.co.uk/celebrating-ada-lovelace/

Cheslak, C. (2018). *Hedy Lamarr.* National women's history museum. https://www.womenshistory.org/education-resources/biographies/hedy-lamarr

Daniels, P. E. (2019). *Biography of emmeline Pankhurst, women's rights activist.* ThoughtCo. https://www.thoughtco.com/emmeline-pankhurst-1779832

*Dr Lilla Watson.* (2020, January 31). The University of Queensland. https://alumni.uq.edu.au/story/6819/dr-lilla-watson

Drugmand, D. (2019, November 19). *Rachel Maddow's new book on russia, oil, and politics accidentally had perfect timing with trump impeachment inquiry.* DeSmog. https://www.desmog.com/2019/11/19/rachel-maddow-blowout-book-russia-oil-politics-trump-impeachment/

Eisenberg, B., & Ruthsdotter, M. (1998). *History of the women's rights movement.* National Women's History Alliance. https://nationalwomenshistoryalliance.org/history-of-the-womens-rights-movement/

*Family tree of Rachel MADDOW.* (n.d.). Geneanet. https://en.geneastar.org/genealogy/maddowrache/rachel-maddow

Freiberger, P., & Swaine, M. (2018, November 23). *Ada Lovelace | Biography & facts.* Encyclopædia Britannica. https://www.britannica.com/biography/Ada-Lovelace

Frida Kahlo and the legacy of feminist ideology. (2022). *Collier & Dobson.* https://www.collierdobson.com/blogs/news/frida-kahlo-and-the-legacy-of-feminist-

ideology?srsltid=AfmBOooIUFc_VMCc1jAhiqd2LkkBn3sSM
RxJ-XROyRb4WdZMqOALqlzZ

*Frida     Kahlo     biography.*   (2002).    Frida     Kahlo.
https://www.fridakahlo.org/frida-kahlo-biography.jsp

*Frida   Kahlo.*   (2024).   Fiveable.me.   https://library.fiveable.me/key-
terms/introduction-chicanx-latinx-studies/frida-kahlo

Gautam, S., Gautam, A. S., Awasthi, A., & Ramsundram N. (2024,
January 1). Citizen action and advocacy. *Springer Briefs in
Geography;     Springer     Nature     (Netherlands).*
https://doi.org/10.1007/978-3-031-77057-9_13

*Hanan Ashrawi.* (2020). Interactive encyclopedia of the Palestine
question          –                    Palquest.
https://www.palquest.org/en/biography/14595/hanan-
ashrawi

*Hedy Lamarr and frequency hopping technology.* (2023, March 8).
Www.sparkfun.com. https://www.sparkfun.com/news/6147

*Hedy Lamarr.* (n.d.). Smithsonian American Women's History.
https://womenshistory.si.edu/herstory/science-
innovation/object/hedy-lamarr

History.com Editors. (2009, November 9). *Rosa Parks.* History; A& E
Television Networks. https://www.history.com/topics/black-
history/rosa-parks

*How to enhance constructive public dialogue on social media.* (2023). DW.COM.
https://akademie.dw.com/en/recommendations-how-to-
enhance-constructive-public-dialogue-on-social-media/a-
67342589

*Iceland women's history museum [in Icelandic].* (2020). Kosningaréttur
kvenna.

https://kvennasogusafn.is/index.php?page=kosningarettur-kvenna

*Impact of the nineteenth amendment beyond the supreme court.* (2020). Congress. https://constitution.congress.gov/browse/essay/amdt19-4/ALDE_00013829/

*Intersectional feminism: what it means and why it matters right now.* (2020, July 1). UN Women; United Nations. https://www.unwomen.org/en/news/stories/2020/6/explainer-intersectional-feminism-what-it-means-and-why-it-matters

Leaders and citizens: Women's political participation in India. (n.d.). *International Growth Centre.* https://www.theigc.org/blogs/gender-equality/leaders-and-citizens-womens-political-participation-india

*Life Story: Billie Jean King.* (n.d.). Women & the American Story. https://wams.nyhistory.org/growth-and-turmoil/feminism-and-the-backlash/billie-jean-king/

*LSE statement on PhD of Dr Tsai Ing-wen.* (2019). London School of Economics and Political Science. https://www.lse.ac.uk/News/Latest-news-from-LSE/2019/j-October-2019/LSE-statement-on-PhD-of-Dr-Tsai-Ing-wen

*Malala addresses youth delegates in UN.* (n.d.). UNICEF Ireland. https://www.unicef.ie/stories/one-child-one-teacher-one-book-and-one-pen-can-change-the-world/

*Malala Yousafzai.* (2017). United Nations. https://www.un.org/en/messengers-peace/malala-yousafzai

*Malala's Story | Malala Fund.* (2024). Malala Fund. https://malala.org/malalas-story

*Marie Curie the scientist.* (2016). Marie Curie. https://www.mariecurie.org.uk/who/our-history/marie-curie-the-scientist

*Marie Curie.* (n.d.). Science History Institute. https://www.sciencehistory.org/education/scientific-biographies/marie-sklodowska-curie/

*Marie Curie's achievements.* (n.d.). Encyclopedia Britannica. https://www.britannica.com/summary/Marie-Curies-Achievements

Marino, K. M. (2019). *The International history of the US suffrage movement (U.S. National Park Service).* Nps.gov; National Park Service. https://www.nps.gov/articles/the-internationalist-history-of-the-us-suffrage-movement.htm

Marsh, S., & Escritt, T. (2024, November 21). *Angela Merkel's legacy under fire as she publishes memoirs.* Reuters. https://www.reuters.com/world/europe/angela-merkel-memoir-recalls-tricks-dealing-with-donald-trump-2024-11-21/

Melville, A. (2017, July). Educational disadvantages and indigenous law students: Barriers and potential solutions. *Asian Journal of Legal Education.* https://doi.org/10.1177/2322005817700202

Michals, D. (2015). *Sojourner Truth.* National Women's History Museum; National Women's History Museum. https://www.womenshistory.org/education-resources/biographies/sojourner-truth

MITRA, S. (2013, October 21). *An in-depth analysis of PM Indira Gandhi's attempts to carry out her campaign promises.* India Today. https://www.indiatoday.in/magazine/cover-story/story/19820215-an-in-depth-analysis-of-pm-indira-gandhis-attempts-to-carry-out-her-campaign-promises-771448-2013-10-21

Moskowitz, C. (2024, October 15). *How Marie Curie helped a generation of women break into science.* Scientific American. https://www.scientificamerican.com/article/how-marie-curie-helped-a-generation-of-women-break-into-science/

Norwood, A. (2017). *Rosa Parks.* National Women's History Museum. https://www.womenshistory.org/education-resources/biographies/rosa-parks

Olsen, A., & Lovett, R. (2016). *Existing knowledge, practice and responses to violence against women in Australian Indigenous communities:...* ResearchGate; unknown. https://www.researchgate.net/publication/293768448_Existing_knowledge_practice_and_responses_to_violence_against_women_in_Australian_Indigenous_communities_State_of_knowledge_paper

*Our history.* (n.d.). The Green Belt Movement. https://www.greenbeltmovement.org/who-we-are/our-history

*Pat O'Shane AM.* (2022). Www.vic.gov.au. https://www.vic.gov.au/pat-oshane-am

Petrikowski, N. P. (2019). Angela Merkel | biography, political career, & facts. In *Encyclopædia Britannica.* https://www.britannica.com/biography/Angela-Merkel

Pletcher, K. (2019). Tsai Ing-wen | president of Taiwan | Britannica. In *Encyclopædia Britannica.* https://www.britannica.com/biography/Tsai-Ing-wen

Professor Antonia Finnane. (2024, March 5). *Taiwan's first woman president: The paradox of Tsai Ing-wen.* Melbourne Asia Review. https://melbourneasiareview.edu.au/taiwans-first-woman-president-the-paradox-of-tsai-ing-wen/

*Rachel Maddow.* (2024). This Resume Does Not Exist. https://thisresumedoesnotexist.com/resume/rachel-maddow/

Rae, A. (2021, November 9). *Women in foreign policy.* Women in Foreign Policy. http://www.womeninforeignpolicy.org/the-zig-zag/women-indian-politics

*Rosa Parks.* (2022). NAACP. https://naacp.org/find-resources/history-explained/civil-rights-leaders/rosa-parks

Rothberg, E. (2021, March). *Sylvia Rivera.* National Women's History Museum. https://www.womenshistory.org/education-resources/biographies/sylvia-rivera

Rothberg, E. (2022). *Marsha P. Johnson.* National Women's History Museum. https://www.womenshistory.org/education-resources/biographies/marsha-p-johnson

*Santamaria, C.* (2021, March 19). Women in power — Taiwan's Tsai Ing-wen. GZERO Media. https://www.gzeromedia.com/women-in-power-taiwans-tsai-ing-wen

Schallenkammer, D. (2024, April 1). The "Grandmother" of indigenous filmmaking in New Zealand. *Meridians; Indiana University Press.* https://doi.org/10.1215/15366936-10926968

Semenova, J. (2021). *Germany's Angela Merkel: What has she achieved for women?* DW. https://www.dw.com/en/germanys-angela-merkel-what-has-she-achieved-for-women/a-59308030

Shahwan, N. M. (2021, March 16). *Hanan Ashrawi: Palestinian champion of women's rights | Opinion.* Daily Sabah. https://www.dailysabah.com/opinion/op-ed/hanan-ashrawi-palestinian-champion-of-womens-rights

Siffert, A. (2024). *Ada Lovelace and the first computer programme in the world.* Www.mpg.de. https://www.mpg.de/female-pioneers-of-science/Ada-Lovelace

*Sojourner truth: Ain't I a woman?* (2017, November 17). National Park Service. https://www.nps.gov/articles/sojourner-truth.htm

Sottosanti, K. (2023, February 21). *A Vindication of the rights of woman.* Encyclopedia Britannica. https://www.britannica.com/topic/A-Vindication-of-the-Rights-of-Woman

Subversive Sweetheart. (2017, September 7). *Feminist artist: Yayoi Kusama.* Subversive Sweetheart. https://subversivesweetheartfatp.wordpress.com/feminist-artist/

*Susan B. Anthony, icon of the women's suffrage movement.* (2019, March 25). Govinfo. https://www.govinfo.gov/features/susan-b-anthony

Tappenden, A., & Shelton, A. (n.d.). Considering merata mita's legacy. *Enjoy.org.nz.* https://enjoy.org.nz/publishing/the-occasional-journal/love-feminisms/considering-merata-mitas-legacy-2

*Teachers notes.* (n.d.). Queensland Art Gallery | Gallery of Modern Art. https://www.qagoma.qld.gov.au/learn/education-resources/mudunama-kundana-wandaraba-jarribirri-judy-watson/teachers-notes-watson/

Tess in the City. (2020, July 24). *Transforming trauma: A day in the life of yayoi kusama.* Medium. https://tesscongo.medium.com/transforming-trauma-a-day-in-the-life-of-yayoi-kusama-22d88c85831e

*The Arab spring and women's rights in Tunisia.* (2013). E-International Relations. https://www.e-ir.info/2013/09/04/the-arab-spring-and-womens-rights-in-tunisia/

The Editors of Encyclopedia Britannica. (2018). Mary Wollstonecraft. In *Encyclopædia Britannica*. https://www.britannica.com/biography/Mary-Wollstonecraft

The Editors of Encyclopedia Britannica. (2019). Indira Gandhi | Biography & facts. In *Encyclopædia Britannica*. https://www.britannica.com/biography/Indira-Gandhi

The History of pride part 2: Don't forget the leaders of the movement. (n.d.). *Www.jcfs.org*. https://www.jcfs.org/response/blog/history-pride-part2

*The Legacy of segregation a sociological history of black neighborhoods in America cultural and community resilience.* (2024). BookBaker. https://www.bookbaker.com/en/v/The-Legacy-of-Segregation-A-Sociological-History-of-Black-Neighborhoods-in-America-Cultural-and-Community-Resilience/8ac26b8f-5df4-486b-8ff4-274f6e4ebbd6/12

*The Untold history of women in science and technology.* (2015). The White House. https://obamawhitehouse.archives.gov/women-in-stem

Thomas, H. (2022, March 8). Historical women in STEM. *Blogs.loc.gov*. https://blogs.loc.gov/headlinesandheroes/2022/03/historical-women-in-stem/

*Trove.* (2024). Nla.gov.au; Trove. https://trove.nla.gov.au/people/1608268?c=people

*Vigdís Finnbogadóttir.* (2020, February 25). Britannica Presents 100 Women Trailblazers. https://www.britannica.com/explore/100women/profiles/vigdis-finnbogadottir

Walker, M. (2021, April 7). Sojourner Truth's most famous speech. *Blogs.loc.gov*.

https://blogs.loc.gov/headlinesandheroes/2021/04/sojourner-truths-most-famous-speech/

Wangari Maathai Foundation. (2020, April 30). *Wangari Maathai*. Wangari Maathai Foundation. https://wangarimaathai.org/wangaris-story/

*Wangari Maathai.* (2011). The Green Belt Movement. https://www.greenbeltmovement.org/wangari-maathai

Ware, S. (2020, May). *Leaving all to younger hands: Why the history of the women's suffragist movement matters.* THE BROOKINGS INSTITUTION. https://www.brookings.edu/articles/leaving-all-to-younger-hands-why-the-history-of-the-womens-suffrage-movement-matters/

*Watson, Irene.* (n.d.). 1993: International year for indigenous peoples. *Aboriginal Law Bulletin.* http://classic.austlii.edu.au/au/journals/AboriginalLawB/1992/52.html

*Who we are.* (n.d.). The Green Belt Movement. https://www.greenbeltmovement.org/who-we-are

Williams, B. (2020, June 2). *How Julia Gillard forever changed Australian politics - especially for women.* The Conversation. https://theconversation.com/how-julia-gillard-forever-changed-australian-politics-especially-for-women-138528

*Wilma Mankiller.* (2024). Fiveable.me. https://library.fiveable.me/key-terms/hs-native-american-studies/wilma-mankiller

*Women* suffrage campaigners: Emmeline Pankhurst. (2024). Parliament.uk. https://www.parliament.uk/about/living-heritage/transformingsociety/electionsvoting/womenvote/parliamentary-collections/speakers-conference/emmeline-pankhurst/

*Women who inspire us: Marie Curie | OHSU.* (2024). Ohsu.edu. https://www.ohsu.edu/womens-health/women-who-inspire-us-marie-curie

Woodham, D. (2017, November 20). *How Yayoi Kusama built a massive market for her work.* Artsy. https://www.artsy.net/article/artsy-editorial-yayoi-kusama-built-massive-market-work

Yang, J., Mufson, C., & Sunkara, S. (2023, June 11). *Marsha P. Johnson's historic role in the LGBTQ+ rights movement.* PBS NewsHour. https://www.pbs.org/newshour/show/marsha-p-johnsons-historic-role-in-the-lgbtq-rights-movement

*Yayoi Kusama.* (2024). Fiveable.me. https://fiveable.me/key-terms/queer-art-history/yayoi-kusama

*Young climate activists demand action and inspire hope.* (2023). Unicef. https://www.unicef.org/stories/young-climate-activists-demand-action-inspire-hope

# Image References

Ada Lovelace https://chat.chatbotapp.ai/?model=image-generator

Angela Merkel https://chat.chatbotapp.ai/?model=image-generator

*Billie Jean King: ID: E0WBEM Keystone Press* / Alamy Stock Photo

Emmeline Pankhurst https://chat.chatbotapp.ai/?model=image-generator

*Frida Kahlo: Image ID:2C6F44W* Dom Slike / Alamy Stock Photo

*Greta Thunberg: ID: 2DEFR9B Abaca Press* / Alamy Stock Photo

*Hanan Ashrawi: ID: 2PYWK7K Sueddeutsche Zeitung* Photo / Alamy Stock Photo

Hedy Lamarr https://chat.chatbotapp.ai/?model=image-generator

*Indira Gandhi: ID: E0YYKT Keystone Press* / Alamy Stock Photo

Irene Watson artist Raden Norfiqri, December 2024

Julia Gillard https://chat.chatbotapp.ai/?model=image-generator

Malala Yousafzai https://chat.chatbotapp.ai/?model=image-generator

Marie Curie https://chat.chatbotapp.ai/?model=image-generator

*Martha P. Johnson: ID: 2GAD8JP Patsy Lynch* / Alamy Stock Photo

Mary Wollstonecraft https://chat.chatbotapp.ai/?model=image-generator

*Merata Mita: ID: PP346Y TCD/Prod.DB* / Alamy Stock Photo

Pat O'Shane artist Raden Norfiqri, December 2024

*Rachel Maddow: ID: TY2TAW UPI* / Alamy Stock Photo. Photographer: Jim Ruymen

Rosa Parks https://chat.chatbotapp.ai/?model=image-generator

Sojourner Truth https://chat.chatbotapp.ai/?model=image-generator

Susan B. Anthony https://chat.chatbotapp.ai/?model=image-generator

Sylvia Rivera artist Raden Norfiqri, December 2024

Tsai Ing-wen https://chat.chatbotapp.ai/?model=image-generator

*Vigdís Finnbogadóttir: ID: E0RTTR Keystone Press* / Alamy Stock Photo

*Wangar Maathai: ID: BNC1BNjeremy sutton-hibber*t / Alamy Stock Photo

# About the author

Stella Renee Stuart has an MA in education and has a burning interest in history, especially in the inspiring stories of women across the ages. She has been teaching for two decades and working on research projects in education. Stella has worked with people from different countries and cultures around the world and likes the different insights and understandings that has given her. Stella has lived in Iceland, the US for a short time, the UK and briefly in Romania. She lives now with her husband and three children in Denmark. She loves travelling and the outdoors.

Made in the USA
Monee, IL
07 May 2025

17019322R00100